WEEKEND
Entrepreneur.®

WEEKEND
Entrepreneur®

101 Great Ways to Earn Extra Cash

FOREWORD BY
DR. LAURA
SCHLESSINGER

MICHELLE ANTON AND
JENNIFER BASYE SANDER

EP
Entrepreneur.
Press

Editorial director: Jere L. Calmes
Cover design: Beth Hansen-Winter
Composition and production: Eliot House Productions

This publication is designed to provide accurate and authoritative information in regard to the subject matter covered. It is sold with the understanding
that the publisher is not engaged in rendering legal, accounting, or other professional services. If legal advice or other expert assistance is required, the
services of a competent professional person should be sought.

Library of Congress Cataloging-in-Publication Data
    Anton, Michelle.
      Weekend entrepreneur: 101 great ways to earn extra cash/by Michelle
Anton and Jennifer Basye Sander.
      p.   cm.
    ISBN 1-932531-58-0 (alk. paper)
      1. New business enterprises. 2. Entrepreneurship. 3. Small business.
I. Basye Sander, Jennifer. II. Title.
HD62.5.A54 2006
658.1'1--dc22   2005027253

Printed in Canada

11 10 09 08 07 06   10 9 8 7 6 5 4 3 2 1

CONTENTS

CHAPTER 2

Part II
GREAT IDEAS FOR
WEEKEND ENTREPRENEURS

CHAPTER 3

CHAPTER 5

CHAPTER 6

CHAPTER 7

STAY FLEXIBLE, STAY FAST: Adapt to Marketplace

Part III
SUCCESS STRATEGIES

CHAPTER 8

REACH FOR SUCCESS: Learning

CHAPTER 9

SPREAD THE WORD: Effectively Publicizing and

APPENDIX

FOREWORD
by Dr. Laura Schlessinger

With all due immodesty, I am probably America's best known champion of children and hands-on parenting. Astonishingly, this has made me controversial. Ted Koppel, of "Nightline" fame, once queried to a radical feminist (oops, didn't mean to be redundant) whether or not she thought that my identifying myself at the opening of each hour as, "My Kid's Mom," was meant to be provocative. Can you imagine? Motherhood and apple pie, provocative?

One young woman once walked up to my signing table at a Los Angeles bookstore, identified herself as a student in a so-called Women's Studies Program, and wanted to know why I introduced myself by my motherhood and not with all my formidable academic credentials; evidently, that was a major discussion topic in her class. I told her that I felt sorry for her if she was being brainwashed to see motherhood as a kind of side-show, but for me, it was the main event.

Being a mother, with the commitment, sacrifice, joy, and frustrations (oh yes, they're there!) is the single most magnificent experience of my life. To have a life created in my body, to protect, love, nurture, instruct, guide, supervise, and support that new human being and to discover a deeper humanity in myself and purpose in life, well, nothing beats that. I'm not the perfect mother; he's not the perfect child—there is no such thing. But the love and bond we have is, to me, perfectly awesome—in spite of the fact that we often get on each other 's nerves (that's normal!).

My son doesn't remember that when he was a baby we could only afford one pair of shoes for him. I remember walking through the mall with my husband and passing a children's clothing store, crying that I couldn't go in and splurge for "cool kid's stuff" That's why when critics try to dismiss me by saying, "Oh, big deal, she's rich—what does she know about it all," I have to laugh. Been there (tight budget), done that (been without).

To be there for my son and still bring in some income, I pretty much taught myself to machine knit (I read books and listened to tapes). I became a dealer, sold machines, and taught privately and through UCLA Extension in the evenings with my husband. Our son, Deryk, would be playing in the classroom or the knitting room, so we would always be together. I remember how cute he was using all the small accessories as tanks and missiles, you know, boy-stuff is in the genes.

I also custom knit suits and sweaters for women who wanted that classy, personal touch. I would do this work after Deryk went to bed or in the middle of the day once he started kindergarten.

Knitting was one "at-home" business; going back on radio was the other. I would take care of Deryk all day, put him to bed at about 7 or 8 P.M., and at 9 P.M. drive to KFI AM 640 in Los Angeles to do a radio program from 10 P.M. to 1 A.M. I'd be up at 6 A.M. to start the whole day over again. No, I don't know where I got the energy; you just decide to do the things you have to do.

I remember being very worried when I heard a rumor that the station might shift me (as a promotion) to afternoon drive— that's about 4 to 7 P.M. I knew I wouldn't take that job because it would mean that when Deryk got home from school there would be no mommy to play with, get munchies from, supervise homework, eat dinner, read books, etc. I was going to have to turn down the biggest opportunity of my radio career—and I was willing to do it without a blink.

Fortunately, I was offered 11 A.M. to 2 P.M., so as I like to say, after Deryk left for school, he had no idea what his mommy did—but I was there when he had to be picked up after school!

I have always worked my career around my family, not the opposite. It is amazing that I have been as successful at a career with that rule, but it's all in how you define success. I don't believe in "balance," because, be honest, family always becomes the last priority. I believe in philosophical and moral "choices." I believe that the choice to make family the first priority gives one a richer, more meaningful, connected life.

When I wrote books, I'd get up at 5 A.M. and work until it was time to get Deryk up for breakfast and school. I'd do the same on the weekends, working early in the morning and then free for family time. Again, I worked around my family. I'm proud of it. You can be too!

When Deryk was in high school, I created my own charitable foundation, providing duffel bags with clothes, toys, school supplies, toiletries, blankies, and stuffed animals for children rescued from abusive and neglectful homes. To raise money, I turned a hobby (jewelry making) into an enterprise, selling my own hand-crafted jewelry on my web site and at personal appearances. Again, I'd work at this after Deryk left for school, before he came home, and late evenings.

I am a big believer that where there is a will, people will find a way. I work hard on my program everyday to try to influence more and more folks to have the will. This wonderful book, *Weekend Entrepreneur*, will help you find the way to be your Kids' Mom or your Kids' Dad.

—Dr. Laura Schlessinger,
author of *The Proper Care and Feeding of Husbands*

PREFACE

Isn't America great? We are a nation of entrepreneurs. Young and old, Americans start businesses at an impressive rate, always willing to take a chance on creating our own futures. Why? Because few things are as satisfying as a dollar (or two) earned on your own, by your own ideas, talents, and efforts from start to finish. The opportunity to create, to grow, to flourish, is embedded in us as a people.

Our nation's history is filled with examples of businesses that start small and grow into significant size. Remember those tiny ads in the back of *Seventeen* magazine for belts and purses? Lillian Vernon started her mail-order empire on her kitchen table, processing orders for personalized belts. If you have a printer in your office, there is a good chance it comes from Hewlett Packard. Hewlett and Packard was once just two engineers in a garage in Palo Alto, trying to make something happen for themselves. Notice the tempting smell of freshly baked cookies in the air the last time you visited a shopping mall? Starting from scratch and extra space rented from a grocery store, Debbie Fields cooked up her successful Mrs. Field's cookie empire.

Some big successes arise from brave souls who have thrown caution to the winds and started off without the safety net of another paycheck. Others, while equally brave, have started smaller, nurturing their entrepreneurial dreams in their spare time while hanging on to their day jobs for financial safety. And many others are content to let their side businesses stay small and manageable, enjoying the extra money and not letting their part-time enterprises overwhelm them.

We've written this book, *Weekend Entrepreneur*, for all of those folks. Why did we choose this topic? Because it is close to our hearts. Michelle spent years as the senior producer of the Dr. Laura show, talking to callers and hearing thousands of stories of people who were hoping to take a chance on themselves to build different lives. She also heard from countless parents frustrated by their lives on the corporate treadmill. So many felt that their own families needs were being neglected as they were forced to let someone else—a boss, an employer—dictate how they spent their time.

One call still stands out years later—it was a frustrated man in his 30s who wept as he unburdened himself on the phone to Michelle. The married father of three, he felt his job was preventing him from spending the time he needed with his family and that he worried his children were growing up without his presence—the very same sort of childhood he'd suffered through himself. Not long after that call, Michelle set up the "work from home" section on the Dr. Laura web site in March 2001, so that parents could try to restructure their lives around their families. Over the years Michelle heard many success stories from folks who had founded small businesses that they operated in their spare time and wanted to spread the news to others who could benefit.

Jennifer herself has swung back and forth from the corporate life as a publishing executive for a huge media company to a self-employed book packager and marketing consultant. As an entrepreneur she has been a coffee roaster, a jewelry designer, and the publisher of both a business directory and a mail-order travel book. With two young children at home, the income she has been able to create on a part-time basis has allowed her to be her kids' mom. When not working as a producer in radio or television, Michelle has also earned her entrepreneurial stripes as a gourmet cookie baker and the owner of a television production company.

As you can see, when we talk about starting a weekend business we are not encouraging you to take a chance on something we haven't done. We want you to join us in experiencing the excitement of taking a chance, enjoying the freedom of making all of the decisions, and delighting in the thrill of keeping all of the profits!

Great as we believe that our country is, the strength of the economy and the employment scene has not been what it could be. Why, at this uncertain time in life, should you take a chance on yourself and start a weekend business? Think of these potential rewards. Some are financial, some are emotional, but all are worth striving for:

- Believing in yourself and being your own boss is a powerful feeling.
- Watching your ideas blossom into reality is rewarding.
- Having the ability to control your own time is less stressful than letting someone else control it for you.
- Having a fall-back position if your regular job goes away will make you feel more secure about your future.

Sure, some folks think being an entrepreneur is a risky step. We would agree. We would also say that it is a risk well worth taking!

Sound like you might want to join us in taking steps to become a weekend entrepreneur? In the past few years we've talked to weekend entrepreneurs all around the country to discover the best ways for you to get started. Some may require a special location, like a tourist destination. Some may require a special skill, like acting. Some may require a special interest, like woodworking. But somewhere in these 101 businesses is one that will fit your needs. Maybe it will be growing herbs, or perhaps renting out "new arrival" signs to happy new parents. You might be interested in starting a small concierge business, running errands and making arrangements for the folks in your area who don't have the time to do it themselves. In each of these business descriptions we've tried to give you a sense of how the business operates, what kinds of special equipment or training might be needed, and how much it costs to start up.

Jennifer is a fan of letting others test out ideas for you. Her first business, a directory of woman-owned businesses in the Sacramento, California-area, was unique to her area but had succeeded in two other communities. Jennifer knew that her business had a pretty good chance of working based on the other two examples. Does this mean you are copying? Not really. You can't copy success, you can only create your particular version of it. If you find a description of a spare-time business in this book that you'd like to try, what you ultimately create will be different from the way someone else has done it. The basics might be similar, but you will give it your own personal spin and make it truly your own.

The best weekend entrepreneurial businesses grow out of your own special skills, talents, and interests. After reading 101 descriptions of how others have done it, you will have the courage to step out on your own with a weekend entrepreneurial business that no one else has yet to think of!

In these days of reality television, starting a business of your own is like a cross between *The Apprentice* and *Survivor*. It takes brains, street smarts, persistence, and creativity to survive on a desert island or in a corporate boardroom. As you begin to develop your own spare-time business, you will discover that you are capable of far more than you ever dreamed, drawing on inner resources and outer muscles that haven't been used in years. Isn't it time you discovered your strengths? Don't wait, begin reading now and start taking steps this weekend towards a small business of your own!

—Michelle and Jennifer

GETTING STARTED
(AND WHY YOU
SHOULD!)

1

A WEEKEND ENTREPRENEUR?
What's That?

"You really should start your own business!" Have you ever heard that from a friend, a relative, or even a complete stranger after he or she watched you in action? So many of us would love to have a business of our own, but lack the time, the money, and the know-how to get it off the ground. Many of us spend hours daydreaming of a life in which we stand happily outdoors on a sunny day behind our own espresso carts instead of sitting in cubicles staring at computer screens. Does that sound like you, too? Don't despair. Perhaps the answer is to become a "weekend entrepreneur."

Owning a small side business doesn't have to be a 24/7 undertaking; you don't have to let go of the steady income stream you have now to get started. You might be retired and not about to embrace the fulltime work scene again. Perhaps you are home with a house full of small children. Regardless of your circumstance, starting a part-time business might be the right fit.

Why would someone want to be a "weekend entrepreneur"? For a whole host of reasons! Do any of these sound like you?

- You could use some extra money.
- You'd love to take a chance on your ideas.
- You feel bored and anxious with extra time on your hands.
- You'd like to find a way that the whole family—kids too—could work together.

In every one of these circumstances the idea of becoming a weekend entrepreneur fits perfectly!

You Could Use Some Extra Money

You have a full-time job, but somehow there never really seems to be enough money to pay for everything you'd like to do in life . . . whether it is a vacation every once in a while or the cool skateboard shoes your kid has been bugging you for, extra money always comes in handy. But are you in line to get a raise at work anytime soon? Sadly, not many folks are nowadays. Is an inheritance coming your way in the future? No? Well, then it looks like you'll have to take matters into your own very capable hands and create your own source of additional money.

Even a few hundred dollars a month earned with a part-time endeavor can add up to a significant sum at the end of the year. Do the math—say you start a weekend business washing windows (because as you know, *no one* wants to wash their own!) and clear an extra $50 a week. At the end of 52 weeks you will have earned an extra $2,600! Quite an impressive raise that you just gave yourself! And if you were able to increase that to an extra $100 a weekend, say hello to an extra $5,200 a year. Not too shabby.

Recent information from the Bureau of Labor Statistics shows that, regardless of the economy, desire to have an extra income doesn't change. Moonlighting is more common when unemployment is low and the economy is strong! Statistics show that 35.4 percent of those with more than one source of income added an extra job or business in order to earn extra money; 4.6 percent do so out of a desire to build a business.

You'd Love to Take a Chance on Your Ideas

You've always been known as the "creative one," the person who gets asked to make the signs for the PTA fundraiser, plan the neighborhood get-together, or come up with a solution to a sticky work situation that no one else can figure out. Or perhaps you are the one who creates the products that your employer reaps the benefits from? At your job you never seem to get a chance to show what you really can do; instead you are always working to bring someone elses's ideas into reality. Wouldn't it be great to take a chance on your own ideas, to rely on your own creativity, and to watch one of your ideas grow into reality? It's finally going to be *your* turn!

You Feel Bored and Anxious with Time on Your Hands

Are you one of those people who just can't stand idleness? Do you need to be busy *all* of the time? Why not put some of that raw energy to work producing extra income?

If you find that the ordinary errands you fill your weekend time with are leaving you unfulfilled, here is your chance to create a small business that will keep your extra time committed and your brain working overtime with the details of a new endeavor. After getting a taste of running your own business, the luxury of watching TV for an hour or two might take on a whole new appeal.

You'd Like a Way that the Whole Family— Kids Too—Could Work Together

Time was, most families would work together in family endeavors. Whether it was plowing, seeding, and harvesting a field alongside your spouse and children, or teaching young children the family trade from the time they could toddle along behind you, families worked together from sun up to sun down. But now we all seem to lead such separate lives. Mom and Dad go off in different directions to their offices, while Sis and Junior head off to school. And when the afternoon comes, the pack is still not together—each kid goes off to music lessons, school sports, or to hang out with friends while their parents are cleaning up around the house, getting food on the table, and checking the Blackberry. This goes on day after day.

An entrepreneurial endeavor could bring everyone together for a few hours on the weekends or in the evenings; wouldn't it be nice for the whole family to work together toward one goal? Wouldn't it be nice to be able to teach your own children about proper work habits and the rewards of hard work rather than having them work at a fast food or retail establishment for someone else? Wouldn't it be great to be able to pass on knowledge, skills, and information that might well help your children succeed as adults in the business world? Michelle takes great pride in the fact that her daughter, Lauren Isaac, has watched her consult with clients over the years and it has inspired her to follow in her mother's entrepreneurial footsteps. Lauren is a graphic designer and photography student who has already begun to attract clients who need business cards, web sites, and CD covers.

Jennifer and her husband Peter both work in the book publishing business. They introduced their ten-year-old son Julian to the rewards of publishing and encouraged him to develop a book project of his own. His idea grew and expanded into a larger project that also included his younger brother Pips, and now the whole family is doing a book together! Check your local bookstore shelves for a copy of *The Gross News: A Collection of True (and Truly Gross) News Stories from Around the World*, compiled by the Sander Family. Looks like Jennifer and Peter just might be raising a crop of authors.

Nina Foster Basye enjoys the companionship of her five-year-old, Lily, as they work together in the flower fields of Basye's Harmony Farm, picking flowers to be sold at weekend farmers' markets. Nina knows her daughter is learning about nature, feeling important about helping her mom, and gaining an understanding of how money is earned. Can you see yourself having these kinds of moments with your own children? Priceless.

Small businesses create jobs at a much higher rate than corporate America. Some estimates place the birth rate of new businesses at a thousand new businesses an hour every day in the United States!

Opportunities Abound

We have noticed a consistent pattern among many of the businesses we've researched. The more successful businesses are often those that have been created to cater to the needs and desires of working folks who are so caught up in their careers that they have little time (or interest) in taking care of many of life's basics—picking up the dry cleaning, cooking a delicious meal for the family, or making sure the windows are sparkling clean each spring. Businesses that sell services to these folks are—dare we say it—cleaning up!

Another phenomenon that opens doors for many part-time businesses is the growing senior population. These folks, for different reasons than the career-focused group, aren't getting up on ladders to clean their own rain gutters. They aren't interested in spending time doing life's little errands and are happy to hire someone else to take care of them. Some of their needs have to do with the physical limitations of aging, others with their desire to live life to the fullest. In the next chapter we'll look more closely at these two markets and help you decide if either of these is an audience that will support your business idea. In the meantime, start looking closely at the world around you in a new way. Notice emerging opportunities to fill an unmet commercial need and then think creatively about how you might fill it.

Have we got you hooked on the idea of becoming a weekend entrepreneur yet? We are both so firmly in favor of business ownership for one simple reason—it is a powerful way to take control of your own destiny. Wage earners earn only one thing—a wage. Business owners, one the other hand, earn tremendous psychic and emotional rewards in addition to equity and limitless potential profits from their hard work and creativity.

Be Honest, Be Truthful

We've been highlighting all of the things a weekend business is; now we need to point out what a side business is not—it is not an opportunity to hide cash and scam the government or any creditors you might already have.

A good night's sleep is a priceless thing, and one of the best ways to ensure you sleep easy at night is to be straightforward and true in your business dealings. Do everything on the up and up and your conscience will rest easy. Operating a part-time business should not be viewed as an opportunity to hide income from the government and behave in a shady manner. You owe it to yourself and to your fellow entrepreneurs to follow all of the rules of business. Investigate just what it takes to operate legally in your area and what kinds of permits and licenses might be needed. And then get them, please. Declare any and all extra income on your annual tax forms, and pay what you owe.

Do You Have What It Takes to Make Your Business Work?

Not everyone has what it takes to succeed in business. Sometimes the idea is flawed; sometimes the business skills are lacking. Before you devote time and money, we urge you to take a clear-eyed look at yourself and assess your own skills and personality.

Among the traits and abilities you'll need are:

- Perseverance
- Creativity
- Honesty
- Organization
- Ability to multitask

Investigate which types of business licenses you will need in your area. Check with the city, county, and state. You might also check the regulations in your own neighborhood if you live in an area that is goverened by a community association.

- Courage
- Self-confidence

If you can not honestly claim at least two or three of these traits for yourself, you might not be cut out to undertake a small business.

Start Slowly, Start Small

Once you identify a weekend business that seems perfect for you, what is your first step? Starting small and paying as you go is a time-honored way to get into business for yourself. Don't go wild with supplies, signing contracts for offices, equipment, neon signs, and business cards that might haunt you later on. It is far better to start on a very modest scale, feeling your way along and gaining momentum a little bit at a time.

You might have noticed already that we are business cheerleaders. You bet we are—big time cheerleaders for the American entrepreneur! But we are also both business pragmatists. We want you to approach becoming a weekend entrepreneur with thoughtful planning and careful steps. Please don't take a chance with money you can't afford to lose. Please don't jeopardize your finances, your children's education, your marriage, or your future in any way. Having waved that flag of caution, let's proceed on to our next topic—how to make sure that there is a market (a paying market!) for the business you plan to start.

2

BEFORE
YOU BEGIN
Testing Your Market

Y̶ou wouldn't jump straight into a pool without learning to swim first, would you? Of course not! Taking big steps requires careful planning and investigation. Getting a business going from the ground up is a bit like learning how to swim. Rule Number One is exactly the same: *Try not to sink*. To prevent your business from sinking, you must first make sure it can float. And for a business to float it needs . . . customers!

One of the biggest reasons that any business succeeds is that there is a healthy market for the product or service. You can spend all the money and effort you want on advertising and getting the message out, but if no one out there is interested your business really will sink. Whether you plan to target busy two-income professional couples, or seniors, or dessert lovers, you first need to determine how many of them they are. It is always possible to target a niche market that is just too small to support a business.

Who Is Your Customer?
Will They Want What You Have?

You will also need to see whether the folks you hope are your potential customers are interested in the product or service you hope they will buy. Few things in life are as heartbreaking as watching a dream wither and die due to lack of interest from the marketplace. Make sure this doesn't happen to you and your weekend entrepreneurial dreams by thoroughly researching beforehand.

Jennifer has logged many hours at weekend craft shows selling jewelry and handmade candles. More than once she has watched the hopeful expressions of many exhibitors as they set out their handcrafted wares in the early morning turn to looks of despair and dejection by mid-afternoon as they watch folks walk by their booths without a second glance. Was it that no one else was interested in owning Christmas decorations made from yarn and old beer cans (yes, true story) or was the price too high on the redwood bird feeders a woodworker was hoping to sell? We all have our own quirky tastes and tend to produce products and services that appeal to those tastes. Take the time to double check to see if others share that same interest.

If you are launching a service for busy moms, talk to several dozen busy moms and run your idea past them in order to effectively gauge interest in the marketplace. Make sure these are busy moms you do not know personally because you will need to launch your business based on solid data, not on the kindness of friends. How will you find a group of potential customers if your friends aren't considered statistically reliable? It isn't as hard as it sounds. If you need a group of busy moms, spread the word to your friends and ask for referrals. Go just one step outside of your friendship circle; you don't have to go any further.

Remember Jennifer's first small business, the women's business directory? You can also find a wealth of ideas and inspiration in the success of businesses in other areas. If the busy moms in suburban Chicago are embracing a particular service, then the busy moms in North Carolina or South Dakota might too. Even if you don't travel much, searching through the business sections of out-of-town newspapers (easily found online) can give you a sense of what has worked elsewhere.

A high-tech way to find out if there is a need or interest in your service is to use a free search term tool. These tools let you know how often people search out the words associated with your business idea. In a later chapter you will read about Jennifer Fallon, the owner of an online business that sells wedding favors to couples. By typing in the words "wedding favors" to "Search Term Suggestion Tool" at www.overture .com, she learned that a whopping 100,000 people per month are online looking for wedding favors. Now there is a hot market!

Sit down with your idea and work through the following process to evaluate the feasibility of your weekend business.

Define Your Market

Who exactly do you think your customers will be? Can you describe them in detail? How large a group is it? How will you be able to get their attention?

Check out www.GuruDAQ.com, an internet marketing experts' index. It allows you to research some of the top names within internet marketing, compared to each other by their online popularity.

Define Your Product or Service

Exactly what do you want these folks to buy from you? How does it differ from what else is already available? Cheaper? Better? More convenient?

Tune In to the Market

Go out and talk to your target customer. Describe your idea. Do their ears perk up? Remember to go outside of your comfort zone and talk to strangers, not friends and family.

Start Your Financials

You've got a product or service and a market that seems interested. Now you need to look closely at the financial side of your new dream: can you deliver your product or service at a reasonable cost? Think clearly about the cost of supplies, labor, or fixed costs you might have to pay. Make sure that the potential profits are justified.

On average, U.S. companies make a 5 percent net income. For $1 of revenue the average company makes five cents profit after paying for all expenses and taxes. Making a 10 percent profit is doing very well, and a 15 percent profit is exceptional. Keep these figures in mind when deciding how much money you can make from your small business.

Join Up!

Another great way to gather information on your business idea is to search out trade associations or business groups where you can meet others in the same line of business. Thinking about a coffee-related business to cash in on our ever-increasing appetite for caffeine? When Jennifer was a coffee roaster she joined the Specialty Coffee Association of America (www.scaa.org) and began to attend their seminars and conferences around the country.

Joining an association in your field will also keep you in the loop on annual trade shows and other professional get togethers. Attending a large trade show might even help you come up with ideas for a part-time business, or further refine the one you already have. We always come away from industry trade shows energized and humming with new business ideas, new information, and new contacts. The drive home goes by quickly as you mull over potential products to launch and new people to partner with.

How do you find an association or trade show? Hello Google. Just type in the description of what you are looking for—"wood working association," "craft industry trade show," or some such listing and see what comes up! You can also check with your local reference librarian for a copy of *The Encyclopedia of Associations.*

Another wonderful place to brainstorm and research new business ideas is in adult learning center catalogs. In 11 U.S. cities (including Los Angeles, New York, and in Canada, Toronto) and 7 Canadian provinces, the Learning Annex catalogs are on every street corner. Pick one up and sit down with a cup of coffee to peruse the classes. Think you might be able to make a few extra dollars upholstering? It can be done—and the place to learn the skill inexpensively is through an adult learning center. Jewelry making, flower arranging, designing outdoor kitchens are all things you can learn through classes at an adult learning center, all skills that could develop into weekend entre-preneurial endeavors!

Too, Too Trendy

Trends are all around us, and a new one emerges every day. Cell phone use, blogging, wearing those little rubber slogan bracelets that Lance Armstrong started (don't you wish you'd thought that one up?), every day something emerges that is quickly embraced by millions of ordinary Americans. How does this help you build a part-time income? By spotting a trend that you can exploit.

Cell phones are now permanent extensions of our bodies, it seems. A clever woman in San Diego spotted a need—where was the attractive little purse that you could pop your cell phone in and keep it handy at all times? She couldn't find one in the stores, so she tracked down the overseas manufacturer and started a side business selling them. Tiny pouches that look like miniature kimonos in vibrant colors, these purses fit both a cell phone and an iPod. Two trends at once! Not only does she market her "Cell Caches" at gift shows and craft fairs, she also encourages teenage girls to market them to their friends at school.

Remember the cigar craze of a few years back? That spawned a number of small side businesses like cigar-related gifts. Around the country crafty women are making and marketing handbags made out of wooden cigar boxes. Later in this book we'll tell you about a woman who has built a profitable part-time business marketing these hot accessories.

> [Success] in entrepreneurship, it is a question of recognizing a good opportunity when you see one and having the skills to convert that opportunity into a thriving business . . . luck is where preparation and opportunity meet.
>
> —The Portable MBA in Entrepreneurship

Knitting is once again a big craze, and talented knitters have figured out ways to make extra income by teaching classes, designing and selling specialty patterns, or creating hot-selling knitted items. In her foreword, Dr. Laura Schlessinger shared how she earned extra income at night while her son slept with a machine knitting business. Perhaps there is extra money for you to make in yarn!

The yellow plastic Lance Armstrong LIVESTRONG bracelets seen on wrists everywhere did spark a number of entrepreneurial knock offs. Keep your eyes and your imagination open for the next big trend, perhaps you think of a way to catch a profitable ride.

Once you decide what type of part-time business you want to start you should write a business plan. Your business plan will give you and others a way of evaluating what you have in mind. These are the items that need to be covered in your plan.

- Executive summary
- Company description
- Product or service
- Market analysis
- Strategy and implementation
- Web plan summary
- Management team
- Financial analysis

For examples of different types of business plans you can review for free, visit www.bplan.com.

Ready to Read More?

Remember, you don't jump in the pool until you know how to swim. Start small, particularly when it comes to producing a product. Start small and test, test, test.

Ready to read more about all of the tremendous weekend entrepreneurial businesses we uncovered for you? The perfect one for you might be on the very next page.

We've divided the businesses into four sections, depending on the business type. Start off with businesses that require you to "pick it up," or put your strong back, hard work, and available time to work for someone else. Move on to businesses that need you to "make it up," by creating and selling products and services. Move into the high-tech world of "boot it up," with businesses that help you make extra money online, and then into the "sign 'em up," section, filled with tons of ideas on designing seminars, boot camps, classes, and other ways to market your unique knowledge and expertise.

GREAT IDEAS
FOR WEEKEND
ENTREPRENEURS

3

PICK IT UP

Making Money with Your Strong Back, Hard Work, and Available Time

Some of the best businesses for weekend entrepreneurs involve using what you have—free time and a strong back—to help out the folks who lack either. Busy working couples, retired folks with less than perfect health, there are thousands of people in your own town who could benefit from having a willing person to help out on weekends. Whether you develop a business as a personal concierge who runs errands and makes arrangements, or a specialty cleaning service that targets recreational vehicles, you can put your free time to work right away bringing in an extra income.

Or what if you also have extra space along with your extra time? Read about opportunities like a U-pick herb farm, a weekend auto lot, or even how to make money from raising bees in your backyard.

Some of these weekend business ideas are new twists and updated variations on old-fashioned business ideas, like offering a nontoxic house cleaning service or a quiet lawn service that won't wake the neighbors with noisy lawn blowers. Whichever most appeals to you, remember our earlier advice—do quite a bit of market research and testing in your own community to see whether there truly is a market for your new business. But dip your toe in first, don't plunge, please.

Holistic Housecleaning with Allergy-Free Products

Did you know that approximately 50 percent of the American population suffers from some kind of chemical sensitivity? Or that nationwide, every single day, 32 million pounds of household cleaning products are poured down the drain? Kind of makes you stop and think, doesn't it?

For some enterprising folks, it makes them stop and think about developing a different type of housecleaning service, a high-end specialty service that caters to clients who want to have someone in to clean their houses once a week, but are allergic, sensitive, or just plain opposed to the idea of all those yucky chemicals. So why not develop a housecleaning service that vows to use only biodegradable, nontoxic products?

For sources, check out your local natural foods store, grocery stores such as Whole Foods Market, or online sources like Seventh Generation, www.seventhgeneration.com. Understand that the products you will be using will probably cost more than the kinds of cleaning supplies you can buy at your local warehouse club, so you will have to take that into account when setting your rates. Your clients should understand though, and be willing to pay a bit more to have someone who understands their needs and interests.

Some natural housekeepers prefer to make their own cleaning products—using a mixture of vinegar and water for surface cleaning and then a baking soda paste for scrubbing sink stains.

A great source of information on nontoxic housecleaning methods is *Why David Hated Tuesdays* (Random House, 2003) by Amilya Antonetti. She founded the Soapworks company as a result of her son's extreme chemical sensitivity, and her products are available nationwide and online at www.soapworks.com.

Is there a need for a service like this in your area? If no one else is operating one, you will be able to get good newspaper coverage as it is a unique idea that ties into a hot topic—pollution and chemical sensitivity. Getting the word out via the media is a great move, and once you have established yourself with two or three clients, word of mouth should begin to spread.

Kids' Coach/Parent Outsourcing

Articles in *The Wall Street Journal* and *People* magazine have identified a new trend sweeping the country—busy, harried, and sometimes insecure parents have taken to hiring other adults to teach their children some of life's most basic skills. How basic? Potty training. Riding a bicycle. Just as hundreds of thousands of professionals hire high-priced business coaches to help them reach the next level of success, they are hiring coaches for their kids. Some of the customers are two-career couples who literally don't have the time to teach their own children. Others prefer to bring in a neutral third party for stressful things like toilet training.

Is this something you could design a weekend business around? Easily. Aresh Mohit is a "bike tutor" who is paid sixty dollars an hour to teach children the basics of bike riding and safety. Shari Green of Buffalo Grove, Illinois, charges $450 for five sessions in which she breaks small children of the thumb-sucking habit.

Here are a few children's skills around which you could design a weekend kid coaching business:

- Bike riding
- Skateboarding
- Rollerblading
- Toilet training
- Basic kitchen skills like baking and cooking
- Sewing
- Knitting
- Manners and etiquette

Are any of these areas in which you had great success with your own children? Perhaps you should start spreading the word about your willingness to help others. To get your business off the ground, start with a volunteer job or two, so that you can find out how well you can teach and what the parents' response is. Once you have had a few successful clients and can include glowing endorsements in your flier or brochure, you can start marketing your skills.

A local newspaper story will also help you find paying clients. To interest the media you will need to have an established track record and several families willing to talk about your help and success.

Teaching children is not for everyone, of course. Not only do you need to be skilled at whatever you are trying to teach, but you need to have patience and an ability to work well with kids. Not everyone can do it; be very honest about whether you really have the knack for it!

Car Detailing

Miguel Milamores, college student and owner of a car detailing service, keeps his customers happy by delivering superior service and taking pride in his work. He doesn't overbook his schedule because he likes to take his time and do a great job for his customers. He says, "My business is not based on quantity, but on quality. It is at your location for your convenience. No more waiting in line at the carwash because the carwash comes to you." Within a few months he recouped his initial investment of $3,000. On his first day he made $250, and if he wants, he can earn twice as much in one day. However, as a student, school is top priority, so he maintains a part-time work schedule, putting in three to four days a week.

Where did he learn the trade? When Miguel was a sophomore in high school, he got a job at a car wash in La Quinta, California. While working there he became friendly with the detailers, and they started teaching him the tricks of the trade. Then, while at college, he did some detailing for employees at the school, and one of his customers asked him why he didn't have his own business. This conversation ignited the spark for Miguel to start his own car detailing business.

While so many people are driven by personal needs, Miguel's family plays an important role in his life. "I have a single sister with a child, that is my fuel! I need to earn extra money so I can help my sister if she needs it. Also, being a business student, I wanted to explore and experience what I actually study because it will help me to identify with the books I read and grasp the concepts with a different perspective."

Although many small business owners have to advertise to find customers, that's the last thing on Miguel's mind. "I can't really advertise because I am afraid I might get too much work and I wouldn't have any time to do it all." When Miguel first started his business, he went door to door with his fliers. From there, it was all word of mouth. It's no surprise that the same people who read those fliers back when he started are his loyal customers today.

Check to see if there are already mobile car detailers operating in your area—folks who come to the house to handwash and carefully clean cars in detail (hence the name!). If the field doesn't seem too crowded, this might be the weekend business for you!

Calligraphy

How is your handwriting? If it is artistic and lovely to look at, perhaps you can start a side business in calligraphy. Real calligraphy takes time to learn, and you can seek it out through adult learning classes in your area, or buy art books that will help you learn the basic techniques. Then practice, practice, practice, until you have a handwriting style any bride would be proud to see on her wedding invitations.

Other potential clients are businesses who are giving out honors and awards to their employees, graduation and birth announcements, or formal parties of any sort.

Hiring a calligrapher can be expensive; your clients need to know the service isn't cheap. Hand-lettered wedding invitations can run $20 each, and hand-addressed envelopes are $6 or more each. Why does it cost so much for hand-lettered work? Because each one is a work of art.

How can you get started in calligraphy? Well, some artistic talent is needed! To find out if you have a knack for it, check out the www.studioarts.net/calligraphy/lesson.htm site and follow the free introductory lessons. Should you have a natural skill and the willingness to go on, you can buy a book from that site or find one at your local art supply store.

To attract clients, take your best work samples and put them into a beautiful portfolio that you can share with your local stationery store. They get requests all the time from brides-to-be who are looking for help and should be willing to pass out your card.

Custom Gardening

Lisa Monckton's childhood on a farm instilled a deep love of growing fresh food. "My family has been farming the same land for four generations, from my great-grandfather to the present. On the farm we use modern agricultural techniques, lots of heavy equipment and chemicals, but over the years my interests have turned organic."

As a hobby, Lisa started a large organic vegetable garden in her backyard to supply herself and her friends. She was so pleased with the results that in 1992 she started a part-time endeavor, a custom gardening enterprise. Many years and many gardens later, her company continues to plant organic vegetable gardens for folks who don't have the time or the knowledge to put in a garden themselves.

Lisa grows seedlings at home in her own garden and then transfers the medium-sized plants into her client's gardens. After first preparing the soil in order to encourage the plant's proper growth, she places the plants close together using the tightly spaced "French intensive method." When planting, Lisa follows the "five Ps" motto: Proper Preparation Prevents Poor Performance. A garden that has been planted by Lisa's methods requires little to succeed other than watering by her customer, who will be delighted year-round with beautiful flowers, culinary and medicinal herbs, and organic produce.

On her initial visit with her clients, Lisa quizzes them about the types of plants they would like to grow. "Tomatoes and garlic are by far the most popular requests," she reports. Most work is done on the weekends, as many of her clients like to learn alongside Lisa as she works. Custom gardening is ideal for weekend entrepreneurs with a green thumb and a love of the soil. Lisa warns that it is hard and dirty work, but ultimately very rewarding.

Her rates are reasonable: Around $5 per square foot includes soil preparation, the small starter plants, and the actual planting. It is up to the customer to water the plants and then pick their own produce!

If you started a custom gardening service, how would you get clients? To attract clients Lisa tried the standard methods of fliers and advertising, with little or no success. "Publicity, that's the best way. I've had articles in local newspapers, city magazines, and radio interviews, and each time I get new clients. As I've grown the business over the years the word-of-mouth has grown with it. Repeat business is a terrific money-maker for me." Lisa thinks that organic gardening and organic produce are hot right now, and will just continue to get hotter.

U-Pick Herb Garden

Another variation on Lisa Monckton's idea of custom gardening is to create a U-pick farm specializing in herbs. You've seen U-pick berry farms, pumpkin patches, apple orchards, and corn fields—so why not capitalize on the huge interest in herbs for cooking and healing by establishing a U-pick herb farm?

This weekend and part-time business is ideal for someone with a large piece of property in a country setting, close to a large town or city. Folks like to explore their region on the weekends, and what better way to pass the time than wandering through a scented herb garden, picking fresh basil for your pasta, oregano for your tomatoes, and tri-color mint for your ice tea? Heavenly.

How much should you charge for your fresh herbs? Check out the grocery store price and then set yours higher. You are selling both herbs and an "experience" to your customers.

Weekend Markets

Establishing a weekend U-pick herb garden on your country property will also give you the opportunity to sell other wares to the folks who stop by. Handmade soaps, lotions, and other items made from herbs would also be of interest, as would country-themed crafts. You might also want to establish a small weekend farmers' market or art fair that happens on your property on a regular basis. This will give you additional income from booth rental or commission on sales that other vendors make.

How much traffic will you need to make this a viable weekend business? You will need a steady flow past your country location to get started. If you have the challenge of being off the beaten path, it will be up to you to let potential customers know that your weekend market is occurring. Sending press releases to your local newspapers (with several attractive photos of the setting to entice them) can result in a story or two that will help inspire folks to drive out your way.

Annie Bowler and her husband John own The Flower Farm Country Inn in Loomis, California, on a well-traveled country road between two historic gold-country towns. Their lovely property sits on a corner, so it has two chances to attract notice. "We have a small nursery and according to county regulations, we can sell anything grown in the same county. It doesn't have to be grown on our land, necessarily." Annie sees a big interest in agri-tourism on the part of rural counties and believes that officials want to encourage this kind of business. Check with your county to see what is required. "In Vermont you see farmers everywhere running their own small stands," Annie points out, "and in Amish country lots of folks sell handmade quilts directly from their houses. I plan to add a line of handmade bird houses from a local man to the things that we have available."

Organic/Quiet Lawn Care

The same folks who are hiring housekeepers who use natural, nontoxic cleaning products may be in the market for someone else to keep their lawns looking tidy without all of the chemicals used by ordinary gardeners and without all of the annoying noise that comes along with leaf blowers and gas mowers.

After a career in a dental office, Christl Saed decided to go back to school full time and needed a part-time business to support her schooling. By combining her love of nature with her devotion to organic garden care, she created a successful business. Instead of a "mow-and-blow" operation like all of the other lawn care specialists, she used a hand mower to cut grass and a good old-fashioned rake to clean up the leaves.

Don't overlook the fact that there are hundreds, if not thousands, of people in your area who are tired of having their peaceful day interrupted by the noise of a leaf blower or a gas mower. There is large potential for a service of this type in most areas, both suburban and urban. By offering organic lawn care instead of the usual fare, Christl found a profitable niche in a mature market.

Running an organic lawn care service is about as "low tech" as it gets. Chances are you already have the equipment needed to go into business later today—knee pads, spades and shovels, sturdy rakes, pruning shears, and a hand mower.

Again, this is a business that will easily attract publicity because it runs so counter to what everyone else does. You could also post information about your service on community bulletin boards, at the natural foods store, or in neighborhood newsletters.

"Rent a Husband"

Not every homeowner has the time, skills, or inclination to fix the small things that need doing around the house. These homeowners are ready and willing to bring in someone else to do what needs fixing. Can you pound a nail straight, replace a broken windowpane, or install a new lock? You might be able to earn extra money on the weekends as a "jack-of-all-trades" handyperson for hire.

Dan Newey worked as a weekend handyman for years in order to make the payments on a rental home he owned. Averaging 16 extra hours a week at $15 an hour, Dan did just fine in his spare time. With his extra income he was able to fund a real estate investment that he couldn't ordinarily afford.

Here's Dan's description of what it takes to make money as a weekend handyperson: "I really only had one or two major clients at a time, but they all owned rental houses and kept me busy constantly. If something needed fixing in their homes, I'd get right on it, and then suddenly they'd remember something at one of the rental homes that needed to be fixed, and it would just snowball from there." Dan didn't have any special training, just what he'd picked up from his dad over the years. "In order to succeed as a weekend handyman you need to be mechanically inclined," Dan cautions. "I found my steady clients by word-of-mouth."

What kinds of small jobs can a weekend handyperson offer? Simple repair around the house, small painting jobs, removal and installation of storm windows or screens, simple plumbing problems, and anything else you feel competent to tackle!

Does this idea appeal to you? To develop and sharpen your basic handy skills you should take courses in basic carpentry and plumbing. Doing work for free or helping friends and relatives work on these kinds of jobs will also hone your skills to the point where you will feel confident charging someone.

Personal Concierge

There just aren't enough hours in the day to get everything done, we all know that. Busy working couples or single parents know it most of all! Wouldn't it be great if while you were at work, someone else could be home waiting for the refrigerator repair man? Or on the phone straightening out your travel plans? Or arranging for a romantic dinner on the patio of a popular restaurant? That need for "someone else" could hold the key to extra money for you!

Ever stayed at a hotel with a concierge, one of those handy people behind a marble-topped desk who would help you find the fastest way to the zoo, or make a dinner reservation, or get tickets to "The Lion King"? You could easily design a side business as a personal concierge, one who doesn't work for a hotel, but offers the same kind of smooth and helpful service to clients for a fee.

What kinds of services do personal concierges offer? Pretty much anything as long as it is legal! Can you see yourself being paid to do any of the following?

- Waiting in line at the Department of Motor Vehicles
- Dropping off and picking up dry cleaning
- Shopping at a farmer's market for fresh fruits and vegetables
- Taking a car in for repairs and picking it up afterwards
- Waiting at someone's home for a repair person to arrive
- Arranging the details for a private party or reception
- Putting up, or taking down holiday decorations

Sound like fun? Except for the waiting part (bring a book), it can be. And best of all, you are being paid $25 an hour as a personal concierge!

Who needs a personal concierge, and where will you find clients? All over. Start by talking to the realtors in your area and letting them know what you can do. Not only might they become clients, they will pass your name on to other busy professionals. Marketing your services in affluent retirement communities can also be successful.

There is a professional organization that will help you get started—National Association of Professional Organizers (www.napo.net). Yes, organizing is also a service that many personal concierges offer! A great book with lots of specific information on how to set up a concierge business is *Start Your Own Personal Concierge Service: Your Step-by-Step Guide to Success* by Lisa Addison (Entrepreneur Press, 2002).

Deck Refinishing

Anyone who has or has had a wooden outdoor deck knows how the weather takes its toll on it after a few years. "Weathering" may be desirable for some, turning the wood into an attractive neutral grey color, but most folks who have invested big sums of money in cedar or redwood decks prefer the handsome natural red color of the wood. Moreover, the weathering effect is caused by a growth of algae, making the deck very slippery when wet. This growth, along with dry-rot fungus, promotes decomposition of the wood in the same sort of process that causes wood to decompose naturally on the forest floor. For the average deck under normal conditions, this weathering process takes its toll after five years or so. It is so gradual that the homeowner might not even notice it until his neighbor slips and falls coming up the wooden walkway on a rainy night!

And this is where ambitious weekend entrepreneurs can really "clean up" by starting a business cleaning and refinishing decks—to the delight of satisfied customers! The homeowner ends up with safe and beautiful decks that will last much longer than those that have been left to rot.

Cleaning decks is hard work, make no mistake. This is not a part-time business for the weak and feeble. In essence it is a hard-scrub job using an oxidized chemical that kills and removes algae growth and dirt down to the bare wood. Commercial cleaner can be obtained at most home improvement stores and at many lumberyards.

How much should you charge for this very specialized homeowners' service? An hourly rate of $25 dollars is more than fair. To find clients for your deck cleaning service you must first target homeowners. Spreading leaflets in neighborhoods is one way, advertising in community newspapers is another, and posting information at the local hardware store is another.

Pet Sitter

At just 17 not only has Andrew Zapatka been building his pet sitting business for the last five years, he has taught his younger

There are LOTS of good reasons to get a job—pocket change, to buy a car, to save for college. Another excellent reason is to "try on" your career dream. Ask for part-time jobs that have to do with your career dreams. Go for the job you really want first, rather than settling. Ask yourself: What are my strengths? What do I enjoy? Is a vocational or college education best for me? What careers are a good fit? Find out about yourself and the careers that may be right for you.

The My Cool Career web site has over 75 awesome half-hour radio interviews showcasing a variety of careers. Listen to streaming MP3 shows 24/7 at http://mycoolcareer.com.

—Jill Sanborne, creator and CEO of http://mycoolcareer.com

brother the business. And on the rare occasion when he has to go out of town for a church function, to play tennis or lacrosse, his brother, who is in the tenth grade, fills in for him.

The idea for a pet-sitting business all started because Andrew and his parents always needed to make arrangements for their dog when they took vacations or went out of town. Occasionally his neighbor would pitch in by watching their dog or he would take their dog to a kennel, which charged at least $25 a day. Figuring his neighbors might be in the same situation, he tested the waters and discovered that his hunch would soon pay off. Andrew started his pet sitting business right in his own backyard charging $10 a day. And for that fee he walks, waters, and feeds the dog, spends time playing with the pets and makes sure he gives them attention so they don't get lonely. And if needed, Andrew will get the newspaper and water the plants at no extra charge.

At the start of each summer, Andrew sends out fliers to remind past and potential customers that he is available for their pet sitting needs. This system has worked well for him from the time he started his business in seventh grade when he was 12

Part-time, student, teen, and hourly jobs! Just type in your zip code to find jobs and apply online! GrooveJob.com is the best source for finding great part-time jobs. Find them at www.groovejob.com.

Another great site, Cool Works®, is about finding a seasonal job or career in some of the greatest places on earth. Get a summer job in Yellowstone, Yosemite, or another national park. Find a summer job as a camp counselor. Ski resorts, ranches, theme parks, tour companies, and more are waiting for you. Let Cool Works.com® show you the way to live out your own amazing adventure! Go to www.coolworks.com.

Snag a Job gives you local part-time job and internship listings. Find them at www.snagajob.com.

years old. And today, he still has some of his original customers. Andrew's clients like the fact that he's trustworthy, reliable, very attentive to their pets, and the cost is less than leaving their animals at a kennel.

Starting a business took some preparation; Andrew read books and articles about caring for animals and what kind of attention dogs need. Some of this he already knew first hand because he has a Chinese pug, Yoshi. Now he can work a few hours a day and make up to $120 a week doing something he truly enjoys.

Mystery Shopper

As a stay-at-home mom, Deva Roberts says, "I was looking for a way to be able to bring home an income while still being able to care for my children. I had just found out I was pregnant with my fourth child and KNEW we would not be able to easily survive on the modest income my husband brought home. Two children in diapers is not cheap!" Deva has always been interested in human nature and is a natural born "people watcher." She pays close attention to detail and as a Mystery Shopper and Customer Service Auditor she gets paid to do something she enjoys doing.

Mystery shopping companies pay shoppers an average of $10 to $30 for completing an assignment. Sometimes they are reimbursed for services, such as oil changes or meals at restaurants. It's a good opportunity for stay-at-home moms like Deva, her children are 11, 8, and 3 years old with the youngest at 22 months old. Many assignments allow you to bring your children in tow. After all, the average customer has children too!

Shoppers need to use caution when applying to mystery shopping companies. Deva says, "One simple rule of thumb is NEVER give money to a web site that says you need to pay in order to get the names of mystery shopping companies because they are only out to steal from you. If you stick with companies that belong to the MSPA (Mystery Shopping Providers Association) you are in good hands as they will not allow a mystery shopping company to be a member if they are not up to their standard."

When Deva started out she says, "The internet was my best friend when searching for information on Mystery Shopping. I did a Google search for "Work from Home" opportunities and stumbled across Mystery Shopping. I was one of the lucky ones who found legitimate sites for Mystery Shopping for free." The more companies a shopper signs up with, the more likely they are to get regular assignments.

"There is no real 'investment' needed at first," Deva says "other than to have a computer with online access and a printer." She already had those things, so she didn't need to put out money in that area. However, you do usually start out using your own money for the mystery shop assignments themselves. Deva explains: "You either request or get an assignment with a company you are signed up with. For example, there are clothing shops where you are required to make a purchase and you receive a reimbursement, but you will not get reimbursed for at least one month later. If you do 20 shops in one month, and each of these assignments requires a purchase of around $10 each, then you have spent $200 out of your pocket. Your payment for the assignments and reimbursement can take anywhere from one to three months, depending on the mystery shopping company for whom the work was performed." Her time is divided between working in the field and filling out reports that have to be submitted before the company she has completed the assignment for will pay her.

After the visit, the mystery shopper goes online to transmit the report to the mystery shopping company, who then edits the report and verifies it for authenticity. Once the editors give the report the final review, results are available via the internet to the managers. With today's internet technology, reports are often delivered to the company within 24 hours of the evaluation. No more snail mail, faxes, or annoying e-mail attachments to open. Since everything is web based, businesses are able to view all their reports in one place, without having to shuffle through stacks of paper to see results.

As a stay-at-home mom, Deva gets paid up to $1,000 a month while she works part-time. She quickly discovered that networking with others in her business and perfecting observational skills is a must if you want to be good at your craft.

Janitorial Services

"Janitorial work is a perfect small business for the weekend entrepreneur," George Bingham advises. "It is very easy to enter the market, and just as easy to get out when you no longer need the extra source of income. And the start-up costs are extremely low; to do most janitorial work in offices all you really need is a bucket, a mop, a vacuum cleaner, and some miscellaneous cleaning supplies. What could be easier?"

George started a small janitorial service some years ago during a slump in the California real estate market. Even when the market perked up again he still enjoyed the flexibility and extra income the nighttime janitorial work brought him. So he kept at it.

How did George get clients? His former football player good looks helped, but so did his persistence. "Get yourself a business card and start knocking on doors in office buildings. Once you've signed and served your first clients successfully, you can use them as a reference to start getting more."

Running a small janitorial service at night and on weekends is a perfect way for a whole family to make money together.

George says it is common to see a husband, wife, and teenaged children all cleaning together on the job. The work goes faster and everyone can contribute to the family business.

Rates are very competitive in the janitorial business. Check to see what the current average is in your area before setting your prices, and understand that the reason you might get your first clients is because you are offering a lower price than what they currently pay. In western states the current rate is seven cents per square foot. George warns that when bidding on janitorial jobs, you should always insist on measuring the square footage of the office yourself. "In real estate everyone exaggerates the square footage when they try to sell an office building, but when hiring a janitorial service they always underestimate to try to shave costs!"

The basic rate only covers vacuuming, dusting, and cleaning bathroom areas. More profitable aspects of the cleaning business are "tags," extras like carpet cleaning or window washing. These jobs are not done as a regular part of your nightly or weekly janitorial service, but rather once or twice a year for an agreed-upon price.

Since the rates among janitorial services are so competitive, the best way to gain an edge on your competition is through superior service. Always be on time, do a thorough job, and leave the office looking undisturbed. This last piece is especially crucial, George warns, because whenever anything is missing or broken, the finger will automatically be pointed at the janitor. Protect yourself by carrying basic business insurance, which will include liability.

Just like in the housecleaning business, there are office clients willing to pay extra for a "green" or nontoxic cleaning procedure. Check to see if this approach might work in your area and set you apart from other competitors.

Rain Gutter Cleaning

It is easy to overlook the significance of rain gutters—until they overflow, that is! Once the downspouts get plugged and leaves and water begin to collect inside, the chance the gutter will tear off the house increases dramatically. Working in the roofing trade gave Mike Ingram a chance to watch this process, and he soon realized that a second source of income was waiting in the gutter. "I learned first by cleaning out my own; that is the best way to learn. Hardware stores sell special scoops to clean rain gutters, and other than a tall ladder, that is pretty much all you need to get started. The taller the ladder, the more money you can make. Reaching up to clean the gutters on tall Victorian homes requires a big expensive ladder, but it is worth it. I can easily make $200 a day doing this."

Mike's rates depend on the size of the house and the difficulty of the job, but he tries to charge enough so that he makes at least $30 an hour for his time. Finding clients isn't hard; he places small, inexpensive ads in the local giveaway newspapers. "My first-ever ad years ago got me three clients!"

"You can definitely do this as a part-time business," Mike says, "but make sure you get all of the appropriate licenses. Being bonded is a good idea too." Once you've established yourself in the rain gutter cleaning business, you might add on another service—installing wire covers over the gutters.

Power Washer

Boys with toys are sometimes the most popular of all, even when they grow up! Ever notice how your neighbors ask to borrow your power washer over and over again? It is a much sought-after commodity. Picture this though, what if you were making the rounds in your town on the weekends for say, $25 an hour?

Power washers come in handy in the spring, fall, and summer in all kinds of ways. Some customers might want you to power wash the whole house before they have a big party or outdoor event, others might want something more specific like just the driveway or the sidewalk in front of their house. Boats need power washing on occasion, as do the outsides of RVs (cleaning the inside of recreational vehicles is a whole other part time specialty business we'll fill you in on later in this chapter).

Running a freelance power washer for hire business will leave you mostly idle during the winter months, so perhaps you can do this for some of the year and clean rain gutters during the cooler months.

Find clients the same way Mike Ingram did for his rain gutter cleaning business, with small inexpensive ads in the local giveaway newspapers. And spread the word to your neighbors that used to borrow your equipment. They might sign up as customers, too!

Window Washer

Years ago, when Mark Miyamoto and two other college friends couldn't find part-time summer work in their town, they simply formed their own window-washing collective and went to work. "It was cheap to start up, I think that is why we chose window washing," Mark recalls, "we got started for around $30."

Mark and his friends spent money on squeegees, several spray water bottles, and a cobweb remover. "We borrowed a retractable ladder and mixed up our own secret window-washing formula. After testing it on our parents' windows to make sure it worked, we started canvassing the neighborhood for clients."

The boys decided that going door-to-door looking for clients proved ineffective; it was too time consuming for too few clients. "Posting fliers at local grocery stores was pretty effective, and even more effective was giving our fliers to local housecleaners to pass out to their clients. We got a lot of clients that way."

Mark has quite a bit of advice to potential weekend window washers. "The most difficult part in the beginning is deciding your price. It takes a fair amount of skill to appraise a job. Each house is slightly different and the windows require different treatment. Those little paned windows take forever! They take twice as long to wash as one big picture window. Two-story houses and houses with high ceilings are more, of course. Our basic rate for an ordinary ranch-style house was around $75, inside and out."

An interesting marketing technique that Mark and his friends used was a follow-up thank-you note. Each and every one of their clients received a thank-you note in the mail a few days after the job was completed. Not only did this serve to reinforce the good work they had done, it also encouraged their clients to recommend these polite and thoughtful window washers to their friends. Nothing wrong with using courtesy as a marketing technique!

A part-time window washing business works best in the spring and summer months. With the bright light streaming in, homeowners start to notice the dirty windows and think about hiring help for the job. Make sure you have your marketing fliers up by late winter in order to catch clients first! Alerting local realtors to your window washing service is also a good move. As houses go on the market, freshly cleaned windows help the house's curb appeal.

Homeowner Referral Business

After purchasing her first home, Debra Cohen and her husband were faced with the unenviable chore of finding reliable home-improvement contractors. Fed up with blindly picking a name from the yellow pages and waiting for contractors who didn't

---

Financing

Bank loans include fees that can financially subtract from the business. Read the fine print before taking any loan.

Family and friends or investors have different issues you need to consider. They may want ownership of the business based on the amount of their investment.

---

show, it occurred to Debra that if they were having difficulty finding reliable contractors, other homeowners in their community must be facing a similar predicament. This bleak reality was what sparked the creation of a unique service which has since expanded into a profitable cottage industry across the United States and internationally.

After extensive conversations with lawyers, business consultants, contractors, and insurance agents, Debra started Homeowner Referral Network (HRN) from her home in February of 1997. This stay-at-home mom used a $5,000 loan, a computer, and a fax machine to start her part-time business. Right away the response from homeowners was tremendous, and after three months in business she repaid her loan, and her gross earnings in the first year were almost $30,000.

Homeowner Referral Network (HRN) is a contractor referral service that helps match homeowners with reliable, pre-screened home repair workers. The HRN takes on the time consuming task of locating and screening qualified contractors, checking to be sure that they're adequately insured and licensed, and serving as a liaison between the contractor and the homeowner throughout the course of a job. HRN services are provided free of charge to the homeowner and contractors represented in the HRN only pay a commission to the network for any work secured.

Debra has expanded her business. She has written a business manual "The Complete Guide to Owning and Operating a

Successful Homeowner Referral Network,©" which documents every aspect of the HRN business for people who would like to start a HRN in their community. You can learn more about it at www.homereferralbiz.com.

When Debra started the business, she worked approximately 15 to 20 hours a week; she now works about 30 hours per week. Last year Debra's HRN business income was over $90,000. She earns even more income from selling manuals and packages on how to get started in this business.

Christmas Light Installer

We mentioned this as one of the tasks a personal concierge could help with, but you can also build it into a seasonal business specializing in holiday decorations. Once a year an opportunity to make excellent extra money arrives—installing and then later removing decorative outdoor Christmas lights for people who just don't have the time or the energy to do it for themselves. Jennifer recently went to a spring dinner party at the home of a distinguished couple in their late 70s. Although it was May, the house was still hung with colored Christmas lights outside. These folks and others like them, busy or not quite in physical shape to remove their own lights, are your target audience.

There are fancy decorating firms who will (at great cost) come in and design a complete holiday fantasy for high-end homes. These companies supply the lights and other decorations that they use. The start-up costs and design talent involved with that type of business are extreme, but a market remains for offering your services to the lower end of the holiday spectrum.

Start looking for customers in mid-November, perhaps even placing fliers on the windshields of cars in the parking lots of stores advertising Thanksgiving Day special prices! Do ask for permission from the store or mall managers, please, lest you get started off on the wrong foot with an important ally. It is best to strike while the holidays are fresh in your potential customers' minds. Targeting high-end neighborhoods is another way to go, as many of these homeowners feel the pressure to put up their decorations early to match their neighbors, yet don't have the extra time to get out there and get it done.

In addition to offering a service putting up holiday lights, you could add a service to the back end when you come to remove the lights you installed. For an extra charge you could haul away the Christmas trees and take them to a mulcher!

How much should you charge for this once-a-year service? A California college student charges $40 for a simple, one-story house job that takes a little over an hour, and up to $75 for larger houses. For these prices, you are using the lights that the homeowner already owns, not supplying the decorations yourself like the fancy design firms. Make sure your clients understand that before you agree to a job.

Holiday Baking Business

Christmas offers lots of opportunities for weekend and part-time business people. It is a time of year when there are more things that need to be done—decorating, cooking, wrapping and shipping packages—than most of us have time to deal with. As a sharp-eyed entrepreneur you know what this means—lot of opportunity to help these busy people out and get paid! One smart woman developed a holiday baking business with one sole product—gingerbread houses.

Like the hardworking entrepreneurs who install Christmas lights for their clients, Cheryl Albers has built a small business around helping stressed folks with their holiday houses. Gingerbread houses, that is. Her web site at www.ginger breadtraditions.com offers seven different models to choose from. Once the basic undecorated gingerbread house arrives, her customers can have the fun of decorating it themselves, with candy and accessories and frosting they also buy from Cheryl. Imagine how much more enjoyable the experience will be for a harried mom and her kids if they can just concentrate on the fun part—making a roof from jelly beans—and skip the hours of making dough and rolling it out.

Does this idea sound only seasonal to you? Never underestimate the public's taste for a comfort food like gingerbread! In 1987, John and Janet D'Orsi started a part-time business similar to Cheryl's, but selling already decorated houses and cookies made from delicious gingerbread dough. They spent weekends at crafts fairs in the New England area and ultimately decided to embark on the gingerbread path full time with the Gingerbread Construction Company store. So don't be surprised if your part-time gingerbread endeavors continue to grow!

Weekend entrepreneurs can follow in the footsteps of the D'Orsi duo and sell gingerbread wares in your area at holiday craft fairs and festivals. As with any kind of food-related business, you will need to have a commercial kitchen in which to bake. Instead of spending the many, many thousands of dollars it can cost to upgrade your own personal kitchen to commercial standards (which need to meet health department rules and regulations) look into leasing time at an already licensed commercial kitchen in your area. Perhaps a restaurant that is closed at night will let you bake in its ovens.

Cleaning RVs

As America ages, RVs are everywhere! Retired couples vacation for weeks on end in their big recreational vehicles, and after returning home are only too happy to pay someone else to clean the RV. Think of this as a housecleaning service, only for really tiny houses.

A thorough cleaning job of an RV will take three or four hours, and you can do more than one a day on the weekends. As you become more skilled and develop a routine, you may be able to do a fine job in less time and include even more customers into a weekend.

Where would you find the clients for an RV cleaning service? Head out to the street and look for RVs in your neighborhood first. Approach the owners and tell them about your new service; your very first clients might well be within walking distance!

You can make up a leaflet advertising your cleaning service and tuck it under the windshield wipers of RVs you find parked in your town. Another great way to find clients is to head down to the local RV sales store. Once RVers purchase their travel-home-on-wheels, they return again and again to the dealer to buy after-market gadgets. Posting fliers or leaving business cards (with the permission of the dealership, of course) is a great way to get the word out. Many of the dealerships have waiting rooms with bulletin boards sporting information about RV clubs, groups, and get-togethers. This would be an ideal spot to post information about your cleaning abilities.

How much should you charge for this? Again, think of it as housecleaning for very small houses, and adjust your rates to the going cleaning rates in your area. You should be able to charge at least $50 for your three-hour job. Imagine, if you can find two or three clients every weekend, the money will add up quickly!

Dog Doo Removal

OK, we confess, this might well be the goofiest idea here in the book. But don't laugh, read on and consider it thoroughly as it is a way that weekend and part-time entrepreneurs across the country are truly "cleaning up."

Yes, this service does exactly what you think it does. What some people think is just an unpleasant and annoying part of being a dog owner could be a perfect opportunity for you. So many pet owners enjoy having their dogs around but don't like dealing with what the dogs produce naturally. Here is where a doggie doo removal service comes in.

Setting fees depends on how many dogs the owner has. Typically, the first dog costs $15 for a once a week visit. A second dog would be half again as much (or $22.50 per week to come by once and pick up after both). To visit more than once a week and scoop the poop, the fee might drop slightly and be in the neighborhood of $12 per visit (or $22 per week for one dog). Establishing a pick-up route of just four or five dog customers a week will add up to a tidy sum.

What do you need to get started? Not too much—heavy duty gloves, a shovel, a rake, a long plastic scooper, and garbage bags. All you are doing is picking it up and placing it neatly in your customer's own outdoor garbage can. If you take it away you could well need a permit for hauling hazardous waste!

The best way to find customers for your service is to post notices in the windows at your local pet and grocery stores. (Ask the owner or manager for permission, of course.) If you are the first in your area to offer a poop-scooping service, there is a good chance you can easily get media coverage for what you do. Free publicity is the best way of all to gain customers!

Scooping poop is catching on across the country, and there is even a professional association—Association of Professional Animal Waste Specialists. You can find them at www.apaws.org.

Cobweb Removal

Another specialized cleaning service that many homeowners are willing to pay for is cobweb removal. Cobwebs are dangling annoyances, often too high up for ordinary homeowners to reach. By offering your customers a biweekly or monthly service cleaning up their homes' cobwebs you will be tending to an unpleasant task that most people would happily hire out.

Cobwebs occur both indoors and out; you can either specialize in one area or take care of the whole property for a larger fee. Style your cobweb service like the pest control folks who always arrive on the same agreed-upon day of the month, do the job, and then leave a small pre-addressed envelope with the bill. Do not, however, offer to spray spiders or wasps while you are up there. Using chemicals and poisons takes this to a whole new regulatory level.

What do you need? Many home improvement stores sell a product called a "Webster" which has a big, soft circular brush about eight inches in diameter attached to a short extension handle. This handle can reach 8 to 12 feet off the ground, but you can add firepower with an extension pole to extend your effectiveness to 12 to 16 feet. Spiders and their webs can be pretty high off the ground!

Like window washing, when setting rates for cobweb removal, you must take into account the size of the house and the frequency of the visits. Charge more for the first visit and then a smaller fee for recurring visits. Basic indoor service on a standard-sized house should be a monthly rate of $30. Make sure you consider the amount of time each client will take, then make sure you are earning at least $30 an hour for your time.

As with the other specialty cleaning services we have described, finding customers for a cobweb removal service can be done with neighborhood leaflets, ads in small local papers, and hopefully, a bit of local press about your unique service once you are up and running.

Graffiti Removal

Graffiti on public and private buildings is an unfortunate fact of life nowadays, but the hardworking weekend entrepreneur can take advantage of this trend by cleaning up after graffiti artists. "You'll never have enough police to patrol graffiti," says Steve Lindner of Graffiti Control Services. "Most graffiti vandals want their mess to be seen. If you get rid of it, they might come back. But after a second time, they'll most likely move on to another building."

Depending on the size of the job, Lindner's fees can range from a low of $100 for a very small job to over a thousand dollars for a larger project. He's found that on most smooth surfaced buildings, the graffiti can be scrubbed off using basic cleaning solvents. Brick surfaces need to be sandblasted with fine sand to remove the paint, and serious graffiti needs to be painted over in a color that matches the building.

Chicago tuck-pointer Dan Webb found that cleaning graffiti on the weekends was a great source of extra income. "This is a great business for part-time people; you can make up to $300 for an afternoon's work. My advice is to tackle small jobs, keep it fast and profitable." Dan suggests linking up with merchants' and business associations like chamber of commerce in order to get your name out to their members as a graffiti removal specialist.

To get started and acquire the necessary skills for this weekend business you will need to offer your services free once or twice in order to figure out what it takes to remove the graffiti. Practice different techniques and using different products until you find what works best, and then go out and sell yourself to the business community.

Face Painting

Cheeks painted with rainbows, clouds, and stars were standard fare at '60s "sit-ins" and Grateful Dead concerts, and continue to show up today whenever an outdoor event occurs. Take a look at the faces of small children at any large public attraction like a county fair or amusement park and you will see tiny Spiderman figures and round yellow happy faces, skateboarding symbols, and yes, rainbows, clouds, and stars. An artist with painting skills can easily find weekend work as a freelance face painter to meet the demands of these young art patrons.

"Most kids ask for whatever cartoon character happens to be popular, a Disney cartoon or a movie character," explains Cathleen Swanson, "so I try to keep current. I encourage children to go for natural things like fish, insects, or flowers. A very popular trick is to paint their entire face to look like a lion or a cat. Kids love it, especially little girls." A substitute teacher during the week, Cathleen works only one or two days a month as a face painter. Summer months are more active as there are more events held then.

"I charge $100 an afternoon," says Cathleen, "depending on what kind of an event it is." A face painter is hired by the event organizer so that children can line up and have their faces painted for free. "Parents love it, and it makes the children feel very special," Cathleen says.

In addition to outdoor attractions like fairs and concerts, events sponsored by city parks and recreation departments may also desire the services of a face painter. Organizers of birthday parties for kids and company picnics also like to have a face painter on hand. Cathleen finds steady work by contacting the managers of large shopping malls and the public relations departments of hospitals. She also pays close attention to advertisements for big events, calling the organizers to inquire about hiring. "Radio stations are also a prime source. They run many outdoor promotions and events that use face painters as part of the entertainment."

You don't need to invest too much to get started as a face painter. Be clear-eyed about whether you have the talent, though, and take time to paint a good many small faces around you for free before you go out and seek paid jobs. All you really need are a few good paint brushes and a good selection of colors. Cathleen likes to use Krylon, a brand of water-based theatrical paint from Germany, which is available at costume and theatrical stores and is sometimes found in art supply stores.

Henna Painting

Although children will always want their faces decorated with rainbows and butterflies, you can use your painting and design skills another way. Another hipper and more current trend is henna painting. This ancient tradition from the Middle East, called mehndi, is much more complicated to learn, and uses far more supplies. Essentially you are staining the skin and creating a temporary tattoo that can last as long as a week.

Freelance henna painters are popping up in many of the same festivals and fairs where traditional face painters are found, but henna is also popular in different kinds of places, too. If you get booked to paint small children's faces at a grade school festival, you could offer henna tattoos at a high school or college campus festival for students who have long outgrown cute animals and long for an edgier look.

Other places to try to ply your henna trade would be rock concerts and music festivals, art festivals, and renaissance fairs. Nightclubs might also allow you to come in and sell your talents to their customers. Henna tattoos sell to individual customers for various prices, depending on the complexity of the design, and range in price from $15 to $40.

How can you learn to do this? You'll find everything you need to get started, from instructional books and videos to henna tattoo kits and supplies, at www.naturalexpressions.org. Or check out *The Mehndi Kit: Learn the Traditional Art of Henna Body Decoration* by Zaynab Mirza (McGraw Hill, 1998).

Remember that your completed product will last an entire week, so you will have to be truly talented in what you can produce. Practice, practice, practice before you announce your new business!

Manure Sales

We tend to think of weekend entrepreneurs as hard-working adults trying to build up income. Well, sometimes it is the case that weekend entrepreneurs are hard-working kids who've spotted an opportunity! In fact, they could be called "entre-manures". . .

Two best friends in Stillwater, Oklahoma, have founded a thriving small business, and they are both still in their early teens. Coy Funk and Skylar Schipper sell poop. Yep, they sell manure as fertilizer. You can check out their wares on www .manuregourmet.com.

What started out as a way to raise money for a school auction has now developed into a much larger enterprise for the two boys. They have agreements with neighboring farmers to "harvest" the dung from llamas, sheep, goats, and horses. Coy and Skylar spread the manure out to dry, and sell the sun-dried product in bags to gardeners for $5 per cup.

Is this a business that could work in your area? If you have access to manure in large quantities, whether from your own animals or farms nearby that you could approach with a poop proposition, you might well have a good business on your hands.

Once you get your hands on the product, who are your customers and how will you find them? Gardeners are your market, and what they buy is already dried manure. Cody and Skylar learned early on that "if it smells, it won't sell."

Publicity is key here, and your local media will be tickled to get a press release telling the story of your business. Come up with a clever name, work up an amusing slogan (the Manure

Gourmet boys claim to be "No. 1 in the No. 2 business") and get to work with a heavy rake!

Beekeeping

Bees are everywhere, right? Actually, they aren't. The bee population in America has been drastically reduced due to a mite, and farmers and growers across the country are worried about their ability to get their crops pollinated. One state agricultural department even gave away free hives in order to encourage more folks to keep bees.

Almost 30 percent of our produce relies on bees to carry pollen from plant to plant, something that few of us are aware of. And where do these bees come from? Some live in the wild, of course, but others belong to enterprising beekeepers who put their hives carefully on the back of a truck, drive out to the country, and rent their hives to farmers during certain times of the year.

Beekeeping works best for folks who live in the country and have lots of land for their bees to roam. Depending on the regulations in your city, you might be able to keep one or two hives in your backyard but probably not enough to generate a healthy rental income.

"Working with bees is very satisfying," a beekeeper told us, "you are helping farmers and people raising natural foods and meeting lots of interesting people." Playing a critical role in the agricultural process and getting paid for it isn't bad either.

The best source of beginning beekeeping information, as well as suppliers, is the web site at www.beehoo.com. It links to a directory of over one thousand bee-related sites. One company in Jennifer's town is Sacramento Beekeeping Supplies; they are a solid source of mail-order supplies and advice! You can reach them at 916-451-2337.

Weekend Auto Lot

For some years Jennifer has envied the incredible business idea of a local college student. Here's what he did and how he did it—and how you can do it too.

Sierra College is a community college with a large student body in Rocklin, California. Along with that large student body comes a very large parking lot, one that is much used during the week when classes are in session but sits empty over the weekends. So, why not use it for something else on the weekends? And so Sierra Auto Sales was born.

Every weekend the parking lot fills up with privately owned cars, boats, and RVs that are for sale by their owners. Instead of risking being ticketed or towed by parking their cars on a street corner or empty lot with hand printed "for sale" signs on the windshields, the sellers know that by paying a small fee to the owner of Sierra Auto Sales, they can legally park their cars there for the world to see.

And the world does come by, in ever-increasing numbers. Once the student negotiated the weekend use of the parking lot with the college he began on a fairly small scale with just a handful of cars. By advertising and also highlighting the street corner with large balloon arches (to attract the attention of passersby), he was able to quickly build a following among both sellers and buyers. Now, after close to ten years in business, the parking lot is packed with hundreds of cars and boats from late Friday afternoon through early Sunday evening.

The amazing thing about this business idea is that the only thing they sell is . . . space. They don't sell your car, you do. The business only charges a fee to leave your car parked there for the allotted time, everything else is up to the seller. Fliers on the car instruct interested parties to call the car's owner directly, the few employees on the weekend auto lot do not actually get involved in any aspect of sales. They are there simply to direct traffic as the cars arrive, and register and accept space rental money from sellers.

Is this something that could work in your area? Is there a large parking lot or other piece of land that sits empty on weekends? Pick up the phone and call the owners, ask about what it would take to rent the property for limited amounts of time. You will need to get your insurance company involved for a large scale venture, of course; the property's owner will insist on it. But if you can build a weekend venture as large and successful as Sierra Auto Sales, it will be well worth your time and money!

House Staging

Have you ever been inside a house for sale, and although you liked the house itself, the furnishing and decorating gave you the willies? Some real estate agents insist that empty houses sell better, it allows a prospective buyer to "see" themselves living in the space when it isn't all cluttered with the current owner's things. "Less is more" when it comes to staging a house for sale, and an objective eye can help cut through the clutter that the longtime owner can't see anymore.

But a few tasteful pieces of furniture do set the tone and for that a house stager gets called in. Terry L. Cardon formed her business TLC Home Staging, to work with real estate agents to rescue hopelessly decorated houses by "staging" them so that they look livable. Sometimes houses are staged while the owners are still living there, but more often the houses are empty.

For several years Terry had been staging houses informally, helping out when friends and family were selling a house. She seemed to have a real knack for it. With the encouragement of local real estate agents, she finally took the step and began to do it professionally.

What does it take to be a house stager? You will need at least a good sense of design, but formal interior design experience is best. Caroline Benard decided to start her house staging service after years of interior decorating for high-end clients. She wanted a business that allowed her to spend more time with her children.

You will need to own the pieces that you use to stage. That is a big investment for anyone, buying an extra set of high end furniture that can be moved from house to house to house. Another way of handling the furniture would be to try to strike a deal with a local furniture company so that you use their furniture on a casual loan basis and credit them with large signage throughout the house.

Where do your clients come from? Stop in whenever you see a "for sale by owner" sign and offer your services. Network with local real estate agencies and let them know what you can do for them.

What can you expect to make as a house stager? Like realtors, some house stagers set their price according to the sale price of the home—1.5 percent. Others bid out each job according to how much work needs to be done. By asking realtors you should get a better feel for what the market can bear in your area, but charging $1,000 to come in and stage a home is not out of the question.

Math Tutor

Frannie Kate always did well with math. So well, that when she reached a point in her life when she wanted to try something new (other than nonprofit fundraising), she realized that her knack for math could make her some extra money. Frannie is now a math tutor with several young clients that she works with on a weekly basis, even during the summertime. The children's parents are so pleased with the improvement that they are insisting she stick around until the children are out of high school!

Not quite the same as the folks who are hiring themselves out to teach kids the things their parents used to teach them (like how to ride a bike), math tutors often are filling in the math knowledge gaps of the parents. Not everyone was a math genius in school, and it can be tough to try to help your own kid in a field you didn't excel in yourself.

How much should you charge? The going rate for one child is $45 per week; if you are helping more than one child in the same house (at the same time, so you are only making one trip) then create a sliding scale rather than just doubling the rate.

One of the wonderful things about starting a side business as a math tutor is that there really aren't any start-up costs to speak of. Sure, you need to get the word out there in order to attract clients, but this can be done inexpensively through neighborhood leafleting, word-of-mouth, and small ads in parenting magazines. Once you've got your young clients, there aren't any material or supply costs to consider. You bring your brain over to their houses and get to work!

■　■　■　■　■

So, Did You Find an Idea?

You've just been presented with 31 ideas on how to make extra money in your spare time, and the stories of successful weekend entrepreneurs like young Cody and Skylar of Manure Gourmet. Did anything pop out as an idea that both fits your interests, skills, and talents, and seems like it could work in your area? Was there anything that could be modified slightly to work in your area? Say, instead of a weekend auto lot like the one described earlier, instead you might be able to establish a weekend used sports equipment swap, or a weekend antiques fair.

Use the basic technique of negotiating to use unused parking lot space on the weekend and see where it takes you!

If you haven't found an idea yet, don't despair! We've got three more chapters filled to the brim with more ideas and stories about the amazing entrepreneurs who've made them work. Read on.

4

MAKE IT UP
Creating and Selling
Products and Services

In this chapter you'll meet 30 folks who have literally made up their part-time endeavors from scratch. Sometimes it is "made up out of whole cloth," like the women who are marketing hand-made aprons! What all of these folks have in common is that they saw a need in the marketplace for a product or a service, and then went out and created it. Sometimes the idea arose from something they wanted themselves—like a small purse to carry a cell phone in—or sometimes a need they saw for others—like the need for a personal kit of manicure implements to minimize the risk of infection. By staying attuned to their needs and the needs of others, they created new products and services that didn't exist before.

Music Promotion

Twenty-four year old Nicholas Love turned his passion, and some early failures in the music industry, into a successful side business that on a good month can net him as much as $7,000. Love is President and Creative Manager of Proving Grounds, an Atlanta-based promotional firm that caters to B-radio markets throughout the Southeast. Nicholas says, "About 80 percent of my clients are top-tier entertainers in the world of Hip-Hop and R&B music."

Nicholas' task is to ensure the proper market presence that the record labels require for various artists or music projects. In addition to music, Proving Grounds works with companies that are looking to build a fan base for their newest product ventures, which may include clothing, books, or high-end merchandise.

Proving Grounds' competitive edge comes from the markets they serve. Many of Nicholas' competitors focus on the glamorous and glitzy markets like Atlanta, New York, Miami, and Los Angeles. He caters to those secondary, yet equally important markets throughout the Southeast such as Savannah, Georgia; Charleston, South Carolina; Chattanooga, Tennessee; Montgomery, Alabama and Tallahassee, Florida. As Nicholas is quick to point out, his focus on B-markets required less start-up capital than his competitors who focus on those large markets.

Love started his promotional business in 2000 after seven years as a struggling recording artist. "Nothing pains an artist more than to pour blood, sweat, and tears into a project for six months or longer only to have it received poorly because no one knew where to find it. After seeing several artists make this same mistake, I decided to take action," Nicholas says.

With a small investment of just $150 to get his business going, it became profitable almost immediately. After two or three months of word-of-mouth advertising, Nicholas Love's company picked up four clients. He invested his money back into his business like most good entrepreneurs, but readily admits he expanded too fast. Those profits quickly faded away and the company operated in the red for quite some time. "Foolish spending can kill the best of ideas." Nicholas wound up investing an additional $10,000 over a two-year period to keep his business going.

Nicholas still works his day job but manages to find time to run his business via his cell phone during two 15-minute breaks plus his lunch hour. He currently spends about 25 hours per week running his business. Nicholas believes his most helpful resource was other entrepreneurs. Talking to other people in his field who were willing to share their knowledge of the business helped his business thrive.

Is there a need like this in your area? If music is your love, this might be for you. Start talking to local musicians to learn more about the local recording scene and to gauge whether a need exists.

Real Estate Rentals

Linda Knight developed a fondness for real estate when she was a young child because of her grandmother. "As long as I can remember my grandmother owned trailers and apartments and every Friday I went with her to collect the rent," recalls Linda. As an adult it seemed only natural that she start a part-time business doing the same thing.

In 2000 she set up BSL Challenge of Destin, LLC, a limited liability corporation. With the help of a fellow co-worker who walked her through the whole organization process, Linda negotiated the deal for a condo she bought in Destin, Florida, under the name of her newly formed company. She worked diligently to build her real estate portfolio by buying foreclosed houses around Birmingham, Alabama, fixing them up, and renting them out.

Starting a business didn't come without challenges and sacrifices. Although getting the time off from her job in order to study for and take the real estate license exam was a challenge, Linda was determined to stay on track. She mapped out a plan and wrote down what it would take to make her dream a reality, even if it meant giving up her own home, renting out the townhouse she was buying, and living with a family member so she could eventually buy more real estate in Destin.

Now Linda has her real estate license, and works nights and weekends for Re/MAX Realty Brokers, Inc., plus she still has her full-time job, and owns several rental properties. Also, she is fulfilling a personal promise she made to herself—she rents out a house specifically to help supplement her mother's income.

Linda offers real estate services ranging from rental to purchase, relocation to vacation, primary, secondary, or investment, scheduling and overseeing contracted work, and pairing people with financing companies who meet their specific needs. Her goal is to protect and help people with their real estate ventures. She says, "I didn't decide to get involved in real estate; real estate chose me. It is easy when you love all aspects of something, and it isn't like a business but an adventure where I can make a difference in people's lives by offering my vision and knowledge."

For Linda, the most effective way to get business is using referrals, networking, and word-of-mouth. Her strategy has helped her secure real estate deals in places like New Orleans and San Antonio.

The housing market remains hot in the United States, and many real estate agents use their licenses to generate part-time incomes while working full time in other fields. In some parts of the country the agent field may already be glutted so check it out thoroughly before jumping into this field.

Custom Frames

Talk about filling a need you discovered on your own! Mark Rogers was an amateur photographer who was considering turning pro until one day he got sidetracked by an observation he made about the framing industry. After doing a Google search for 13-by-19-inch frames, he was convinced that there was a niche market waiting to be serviced.

Turns out most frame companies were not making it easy for photographers to buy the size frames they needed. With the popularity of digital photography Mark says, "I was frustrated with the lack of 13-by-19-inch frame and other print sizes from the usual suppliers." He also found it hard to find standard-size frames that would help reduce fading and not cause yellowing. So he started to manufacture and sell gallery style picture frames to fine art photographers.

Mark's company, www.framedestinations.com, markets a variety of products including acid-free, conservation-quality frames in wood or metal, complete with CYRO acrylic glazing and Artcare-treated Bainbridge matt/mount components.

Mark tried juggling his day job but it got to a point where he couldn't afford the toll all the hours were taking on his health so he eventually had to quit. He says, "That got old and I was starting to get burned out. Hard to say how much I work now. I mix business and pleasure quite a bit now. For instance, when I go to a photographer's gallery reception, I view the work, socialize, and enjoy hors d'oeuvres, but I am working and some of the attendees are people I do business with and others are potential clients."

With an investment of $30,000 Mark's framing business was cash-flow positive in about six months. It has been his longtime dream to be his own boss. Hiring one part-time contract employee has helped him meet the demands of his busy operation. Mark had seriously contemplated opening a photography business, until he realized that although he would be running his own company, he would still be performing the manual activities. Instead, he wanted to build a company that would be an asset, one that would produce income even if he was not working and that would allow him to retire.

Frame Destinations is just one of thousands of homebased picture frame businesses. Compared to other frame businesses Mark says, "Mine is a high-volume wholesale version so it is not an easy one to start at home, but it can't last in a home. Regular custom picture framing is a common household business. You can get the distributors to do a lot of the frame and mat cutting so you don't need as much equipment and you can just do the final assembly in your home." The advantage of homebased picture framing businesses is that they have low overhead which makes it easier for them to compete with big companies like Michaels.

The internet has been an important resource for Mark to build his customer base. He enjoys helping photographers in online forums. "People would post questions about where to get frames and I would help them. Now that photographers know me they recommend my company to others." He also uses Google ad words and a couple of banner ads to attract customers.

Manufacturer's Representative

Ellen Gaver worked full-time all of her adult life, so by the time her son turned six years old she was ready to leave her career to become a full-time stay-at-home mom. Her original plan was to take the summer off and spend it with her son and then find a part-time job when school started. It was also very important to Ellen to work in her son's classroom, go on his fieldtrips, and to be involved at his school. However, she quickly discovered that the jobs that were available would not allow her to have the flexibility she needed. That realization is what prompted Ellen to start looking for ways to generate an income from home.

One of Ellen's long-time interests is wellness and prevention. She has always been health-minded, mainly because of her family's health problems. Three of her grandparents died of cancer, one died from lung disease, and her father was a cancer survivor who later died from heart disease. With so many health concerns, Ellen did a great deal of research about environmental influences on health (and illnesses), and concluded that if she didn't make some changes, she would be right in line to follow along the same path as her father and grandparents.

Slo County Moms was started so that Ellen could share a line of products she believed in with others, and at the same time create a part-time income for herself and her family. She is involved with a company that sells affordable, nontoxic household and personal care products. The manufacturing company she buys wholesale from is very unique in that it does not retail products in any outlet. Nor does it have distributors or people selling its products to others. The company sells directly to customers, and in addition to purchasing at wholesale, they allow customers to refer other people who want to open a wholesale account. Everyone wins in this business model because whoever referred that customer is paid a residual income for the life of the account. Customers buy products as long as they like, or they can refer new customers and build a residual income to whatever level they desire. Ellen's business became profitable almost immediately as the investment to get started was minimal.

Most of the marketing for Slo County Moms is done online, and so far it has been the most effective way to attract customers. In addition, Ellen runs local ads and distributes press releases to create a buzz about her company.

Ellen says, "I formed a group of moms and dads whose goals are financial stability and a healthy environment for our families. We work together as a team setting up wholesale accounts for new customers and mentoring people who want to achieve their own success through our business model. By teaching people how to do what we've done, it strengthens our team, insures our success, and everyone wins." If you'd like to learn more about Ellen's business idea, check out her web site at www.slo countymoms.com.

Women's Loungewear

Looking back, 26-year-old Noelle Silberbauer candidly admits, "If anyone had told me back in college that this is what I would end up doing, I would have said 'no way!'" Full of enthusiasm and a great looking line of T-shirts, Noelle's winning formula is simple—great customer service and word-of-mouth advertising.

As a 2000 graduate of Villanova University with a double major in accounting and finance, Noelle realized she needed a creative outlet in her life. Coaching a high school dance team four nights a week while working at an accounting firm led her to find her true passion. Even Noelle was surprised at how quickly her idea became a business. "While coaching the dance team, I loved experimenting with the girls' costumes by embellishing them with Swarovski crystals. Eventually I started to put them on all of my own clothes and make T-shirts, tanks, and undie sets for my friends as gifts. Once they started wearing the clothing, I began getting e-mails and phone calls from their co-workers and friends, asking if they could purchase similar items from me." In November of 2003 Noelle officially started her own women's clothing company, called In Your Skivvies, and designed and launched the web site www.inyour skivvies.com.

Noelle struck gold, and her investment of $50,000 was recouped in 18 months. This year she is on track for her sales to double. Her idea fulfilled a need women have to wear some-thing wild on a Friday night and to own sexy undies that define comfort and encompass all that is glamorous and girly. Noelle adds, "Skivvies girls love to be the center of attention, and these sassy tanks always get noticed. The inspiration for most of the designs are usually derived from experiences that we have with our friends. With Skivvies you can flirt without saying a word and turn heads as the light catches the crystals. Our philosophy is to provide every self-proclaimed Rockstar with a little bit of fun fashion."

Another thing that gives Noelle's designs an edge is that every item is made to order. For instance if an item on the web site is pink with silver crystals, the customer has the option to choose any color combination she would like from drop-down menus.

For Noelle, working at one of the Big 4 accounting firms and running her own company has been nothing short of a small per-sonal miracle, especially during the winter (which is busy season for the firm *and* holiday gift time for Skivvies). The real trick for her is not letting on to anyone that she runs a company on the side. She employs local college kids to help service her wholesale clients and to fill 30 to 50 retail orders each week.

"I look like Santa Claus every morning on my way to the office as I stop by the Post Office to mail out the day's packages. Sleeping in on weekends, working out, and watching TV are lux-uries I haven't experienced since before I started the company . . . but I am so driven to succeed and make my brand national, that it barely even crosses my mind anymore. There isn't one thing in my entire life that has been more rewarding than a compliment from a customer. I think how far I've come, how much work I've put into this and what I've accomplished, and I have to refrain from patting my own back."

Clothing and Accessories Designer

At 15, Taylor Grabiner has already learned to follow her passion. Taylor says, "I love fashion and always have. As a kid, I was always drawing on corners of newspapers or designing clothes, and once I saved up enough money, I taught myself how to sew and just started producing clothing and handbags and going into stores asking if they would sell my stuff, and they loved it!"

Taylor makes earrings, handbags, and clothing. What gives her an edge is that they are all one-of-a-kind designs. She started out designing several pairs of earrings priced at $6 and $7, took them to school, and on her first day came home with $192. Although her investment of $70 turned into instant profits, it took her almost a year before her clothing and handbags were moneymakers. The cropped T-shirts retail for $60 to $90, and handbags, depending on size and fabric, are $30 to $60.

Some of Taylor's handbags are reversible; one side usually has a pattern and the other side is solid, in cotton or satin fabric. Her schoolmates and friends frequently get compliments when they carry her bags, and this has been the source of a lot of free publicity for Taylor.

Along with hobbies like cooking and surfing, she makes time for her high school dance team and performs at all of their varsity basketball and football games. Taylor spends one to three hours a day designing new fashions and working on her business.

Many creative people daydream about how cool it would be to become a fashion designer. Taylor didn't just dream about it, she sat down and made it happen. Many handmade items found in fashion boutiques come from creative artists who are producing

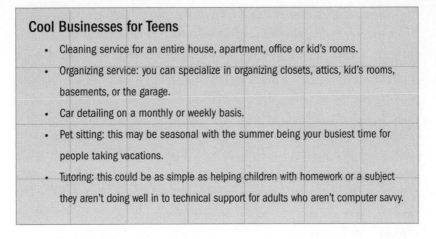

Cool Businesses for Teens

- Cleaning service for an entire house, apartment, office or kid's rooms.
- Organizing service: you can specialize in organizing closets, attics, kid's rooms, basements, or the garage.
- Car detailing on a monthly or weekly basis.
- Pet sitting: this may be seasonal with the summer being your busiest time for people taking vacations.
- Tutoring: this could be as simple as helping children with homework or a subject they aren't doing well in to technical support for adults who aren't computer savvy.

their wares on a part-time basis. If this is your dream too, start making samples and knocking on doors. Once you gain confidence from the first sale, you will hold your head high when approaching the next potential account.

Mobile DJ and Event Planning

Muscle Man Music, a mobile DJ and event planning company is the brainchild of husband-and-wife team Jason and Kerri Christopher. According to Kerri, "We were tossing around ideas for names and since we are both into exercise and Jason works out quite a bit, I came up with Muscle Man Music. We have found that it is a name that stands out and is easy to remember." You can see their web site at www.muscleman music.com.

One day Kerri attended a wedding Jason was DJing; she was inspired and they started brainstorming ways they could combine their talents to ensure a successful and memorable event for the client and their guests and from there, Muscle Man Music was conceived. The learning curve was small because they already had the right training and skill set from past jobs in radio and event planning.

Jason and Kerri were both motivated to start their own business from the desire to do their own thing. They wanted to take the best of their talents and put them together to create a successful business. They are a dynamic duo and their company is a full-service DJ/Emcee/Event Planning company, from tables, chairs, and tents to bouncers, concessions, and much more. Jason has more than 14 years of DJ and Emcee experience including television and radio work, and Kerri has spent five years as an event planner and provides professional coordinating from inception to completion. With all these complimentary talents, the couple's $6,000 investment on equipment (they already had a well-stocked CD collection) helped the business turn a profit within seven months. Their schedule varies but they work 10 to 20 hours a week, which adds up to $2,500 extra in income monthly. They don't advertise and they get clients through referrals.

The newlyweds say it was clearly the right decision, "It has been a great experience. Most couples do not get a chance to work with each other let alone at something that they both enjoy doing. Yes, there are challenges here and there but to work with your best friend is the greatest reward."

You can find the specific information you need in *Start Your Own Event Planning Business: Your Step-by-Step Guide to Success* by Krista Turner (Entrepreneur Press, 2004).

Backpack Designer and Manufacturer

Here is another great idea that arose out of someone's own need. Laura Udell is a devoted wife and mother who takes her role as protector of her three children seriously. Concerned about the health risks her kids were facing from carrying their heavy backpacks full of school books, she intuitively knew there was a healthy alternative. She soon discovered that she wasn't alone, and that parents around the world are struggling with the same issue. Her quest led to the forming of ZÜCA (www.zuca.com), which stands for "Zee Ultimate Carry-All" and her company is dedicated to creating healthy products for people on the go.

Back pain is the second leading cause of medical complaints in the United States, and the rate of back pain and injury in children is now equal to the number of adult sufferers. Laura's fear, that we are raising a generation of children who will suffer with chronic back problems as adults, drove her to recruit her engineer husband, Nick, to help her come up with a solution. The result is a line of high quality products that fuse fashion, function, and fun.

What Laura has created is the ultimate activity carry-all, and the only rolling bag on the market with an integrated seat or gear platform that allows you to sit on it. Engineered to perfection, ZÜCA has a silent dual wheel system for easy stair or curb climbing, an interchangeable inner bag that allows you to change your bag as often as you change your outfit, and allows ZÜCA to virtually last forever. Laura began working on ZÜCA in 1998, incorporated in 2003, and entered the market July 2004. Using a hefty amount of personal funds as well as outside investments, year two revenue is projected to be more than $2 million.

Brand new to the market, and available at major retailers like Nordstrom, this is one of the most unique and cool bags ever. ZÜCA was recently presented as the gift bag of the *Entertainment Weekly* Emmy pre-party and as the "high roller" gift bag for the 2004 Radio Music Awards in Las Vegas. Recipients include A-list celebs such as Paris Hilton, Nicole Richie, Lindsey Lohan, Taye Diggs, and Bijou Phillips.

According to Laura, being media savvy isn't the only way to play the game, "Word-of-mouth or viral marketing has been very strong for us. Our customers love our products and love to send people to us. It's a slower growth model, but I think will build a stronger foundation in the long run."

Custom Gift Baskets

Cynthia Wade makes gift baskets in her spare time but they are not the run-of-the-mill baskets seen in stores and boutiques. She is quick to explain why her product stands out in a world of copy cats: "I don't actually use baskets, I use beautiful ceramic bowls that I pick up from various places, no two are ever alike. Second, I ask very detailed questions about the recipient's personality, age, likes, dislikes, and come up with something unique to them. Third, I design brand-name gift baskets, theme baskets, and seasonal baskets. Fourth, I design baskets for a more mature market—baby boomers 45 to 60 years old. My baskets are high-end, yet affordable."

Five years ago when everyone started asking Cynthia to design a basket for them or as a gift, her company, Cynthia's Custom Basket Creations (www.basketsbycynthia.com) was born. She has always loved to create beautiful gift baskets, and it soon became seasonal and part-time income on weekends and around holidays. For Cynthia, finding her passion came from simply following her creativity and fondness for creating beautiful things for friends and family. The income automatically followed.

While many new companies struggle to turn a profit, from day one Cynthia made money from her initial investment of less than $1,000. She credits her beginner's luck to shopping at discount stores. She also had a knack for finding one-of-a-kind ceramic bowls as well as the items to put into the baskets. She quickly learned to anticipate the needs of her clientele and was always finding unique things.

Cynthia is employed full time and doesn't have any plans to quit her day job. How does she spread the word on her products? "My most effective marketing strategy is referral partners who own businesses frequented by women. Next, other happy clients, and of course, my family and friends are frequent customers. Also, displaying baskets around holidays in places where women are known to hang out like nail salons, spas, and hair salons."

How can you get started in the gift basket field? Check out *Start Your Own Gift Basket Service* by Jacquelyn Lynn (Entrepreneur Press, 2003). A great way to distinguish yourself from competitors is to find a basket niche—perhaps no one in your area is doing a cookie basket, or a basket filled with goodies all produced locally, or a book-themed basket. Be as inventive as you can to create your own special niche.

Cigar Box Handbags

Shawn Lively, a stay-at-home mom, struck gold when she launched her smokin' hot designs. From the nostalgic name of her company, "Charmed I'm Sure," to the elegant cigar box purses she designs, Shawn's handbags swiftly started turning heads far beyond her 78731 Austin, Texas, zip code. It all started when a friend who worked for a cigar company gave her a bunch of cigar boxes and Shawn set to work figuring out a way to use them. Now she enjoys running a part-time business that brings in an additional $45,000 a year.

Shawn began by creating purses for herself with images of her favorite things. It wasn't long before her handbags became a hit with everyone she knew. Customers were ordering her handbags as soon as they saw them and what was once a hobby quickly turned into a business offering one-of-a-kind handbags.

One of the highly effective strategies Shawn used to market her product was immediately hiring a public relations person to get her name out to television stations, magazines, and newspapers. Next, boutiques all over the country were ordering these "must-have" purses for their customers.

As the demand grew, Shawn recognized that she needed help. A recent graduate from the University of Texas, Andrea Hicks, became her partner. Together they have grown the business even larger, and run the busy web site at www.charmedimsurebou tique.com.

What makes these handbags unique is that any image can be transferred to any cigar box. If someone wants a specific photograph (children, dogs, grandchildren, wedding, or best friends), they can have it. Shawn's goal was to create a cigar box purse that people would be proud to show off and that would last.

Their cigar box purses are high quality, with special accessories like handblown vintage glass beads that are placed on solid brass handles. Each purse is coated several times with a triple-thick gloss to protect and preserve it. Unique matching tassels are selected for each box and they use only solid brass corners and hasps. They create the images and then they are embellished with jewels to add a chic finishing touch. Each purse is handmade, one at a time, and they will never make the same purse twice. Shawn cautions clients because these purses will attract tons of attention (mostly from the opposite sex).

For more ideas on how to start a business selling your own handmade crafts, check out *Start Your Own Crafts Business: Your Step-by-Step Guide to Success*, by Jacquelyn Lynn (Entrepreneur Press, 2003).

ID Kits for Children

Like many stay-at-home mothers, Lynnette Scott wanted to have her own business. However, she never dreamed it would take three years to finally find the right one, "I happened to pick up a local magazine that I had never really looked at before and noticed a very small advertisement in the corner of a page that was announcing a Work at Home Fest, which mentioned something about Child Safety. Being a mom and an educator, I knew I had to go check it out. I met with a gal that was selling My Precious Kid ID products and instantly knew that it was what I was looking for. I had to do some research and make sure that it was going to work for me, so I signed up to become a rep for this company."

The amount to get started was only $50 but Lynette spent a little more money to get up and running quickly. She works an average of 20 hours a week and having a flexible schedule allows her to focus her time on her four-year-old son and family. Her future plan is to put more time into her business once her son starts school.

There are several ways Lynnette markets her products, from handing out brochures, catalogs, safety information, and business cards to telling everyone she meets about IDKits4Kids. Brochure racks are set up in different places, she has her own web site, and her contact information is on everything she hands out to potential customers.

However, Lynnette's favorite way to market her line of safety products is by doing vendor fairs, events, and safety classes. Earnings from a one-day vendor fair or event can range from $100 to $400. Safety classes usually cost participants $15; with only ten people enrolled she can make $150 plus additional money for the products purchased.

IDKits4Kids (www.idkits4kids.com) is dedicated to helping parents keep their children safe in an unsafe world. They offer parents the opportunity to buy products like ID/DNA/ Fingerprint kits, first-aid kits, wearable IDs such as medical scopes, ID bracelets, shoe stickers, safety games, videos, and activity packs. With these products, parents have peace of mind and will be able to protect their kids by making sure they have a physical ID on them whenever they leave the house. Lynette says "I love to talk to parents about the importance of child safety and give them the opportunity to keep their kids safe; I market a product I really believe in and it makes it very easy to talk to people about it." Check out their web site, this could be a part-time business with a message you would also embrace.

Restaurant Owner

Running a restaurant is seldom a part-time pursuit, but restaurant owner John Roberts works full time a captain for Delta Airlines. In his spare time he helps his wife run their casual dining establishment, The Ottsville Inn in Upper Bucks County, Pennsylvania (www.ottsvilleinn.com).

John recalls how the events of 9/11 threw his industry into complete turmoil; over 1,000 Delta pilots were laid off and the future was uncertain. His family decided that while he still had a steady paycheck coming in, it would be the perfect time to start another venture. Trying to think of a way to support his wife and their four children, John and his wife stumbled upon a local neighborhood restaurant with retiring owners. With little experience and a ton of ignorance, they entered the restaurant business in November of 2003.

Their immediate challenge was that the prior owners had never made much of a profit, and even worse, the restaurant's food had a dubious reputation. Clearly they needed a new idea, and fast! They now fly fresh fish in from the Pacific Northwest that was purchased from Pike's Place Market. John says "We used the uniqueness of our "procurement methods" in our advertising and in two years have become the go-to seafood house in Bucks County. Last month, March, typically a slow month, we had the best month ever, with sales topping $45,000 and we are looking for an additional site to expand."

John and his wife invested approximately $30,000 and a whole lot of sweat equity in the beginning. Other family members contributed around $25,000. Throughout the first two years there were several times they had to raid their personal family account for various expenses, payroll, rent, etc., but the restaurant has prospered quite nicely.

During the rough times, books on perseverance and having others involved in the process helped them. John says "We questioned our move many times in the first two years but there was always one of us who was the "cheerleader" and got the rest of us back on track. We have also found the local chamber of commerce helpful."

John advertises in the local paper and has found that the ads get noticed and are more effective when they change something in the ad each week. In fact, patrons of the restaurant frequently comment about the cleverly written ads.

Last but certainly not least, John and his wife have established a "community footprint" by giving back to the community; they host charity dinners and participate in other charity events. Running a restaurant while holding down a time-consuming full-time job can make life hectic, but it can pay off!

Operating a restaurant, fulltime or part time, takes a healthy combination of other people and sometimes other money. Entrepreneur has a great audiotape available on the topic—*How to Start a Restaurant and Five Other Food Businesses: Your Step-by-Step Guide to Success.*

Decorative Car Magnets

Stuck in his car in another rush hour traffic commute to work, Wickham Irwin's creative juices started flowing. Realizing that our cars have become a reflection of our personalities he turned an existing product into car decorations similar to the popular "Support Our Troops" ribbon magnets. Turning a profit of more than $10,000 with his first order confirmed that he and his business partner were on the right track.

By day Wickham works as a freelance assistant director in commercial television production and his partner is a freelance prop master for TV commercials. Evenings, weekends, and days off are often used to work in their decorative car magnet business.

Wickham's Stickems (www.stickems.biz) offers crazy designs like pumpkin heads, Christmas light bulbs, chili peppers, hearts, and a bunch of other cool designs. All this while juggling a day job, keeping his stay-at-home wife and their three young kids happy and donating a portion of his profits to organizations like Elizabeth Glaser's Pediatric AIDS Foundation.

How did he get started? Five years ago Wickham invented some flexible magnets that looked like Christmas light bulbs. The bulbs themselves are made from highly reflective safety vinyl. The effect is the appearance of a strand of Christmas light bulbs on your car that appear to light up when the headlights of other cars strike them. Through the helpful guidance of a book called *Bringing Your Product to Market* by Don Debelak (Wiley, 2005) and articles within *Entrepreneur* magazine, they decided to take a shot at a side business.

They got the business up and running by packaging their prototypes and sending them out to their mailing list. The very first sale was a direct result of an article in the May 2000 issue of *Entrepreneur* magazine, which recommended that inventors market to catalogs; they tried it and it worked.

Next, they began lining up vendors and organizing production. The idea quickly caught on and sales began to snowball so they added more product lines. They've been learning and growing ever since. Wickham's Stickems now deals with catalog companies, including several online catalogs, charitable organizations, and marketing groups, and they have their own web site from which they market their items.

Stickems magnets were profitable after the first year. But the truth of the matter is that the first full year of existence was spent researching vendors and making prototypes. Personal investments were minimal—mostly time. The first sales came in 2001—before they were even in production they landed their first catalog sale prior to having all their vendors. The initial capital outlay was $12,000, but that was front money for production for the first customer order.

Once the first invoice was paid they were close to even on their initial investment, easily turning a small profit that first year. Both Wickham and his partner continue to maintain their day jobs, as the buisness is flexible enough for them to juggle both at the same time.

Lavender Specialty Products

Isn't the smell of lavender heavenly? What was once an obscure flowering herb has come into its own in the last decade due to the public's interest in all things French Provincial as well as the explosion of interest in herbs and aromatherapy.

Renee Charleston started her company, Charleston Lavender Farm, as a way to indulge her love for lavender. Noticing the new trend in retail stores like Restoration Hardware for high-priced cleaning products with pleasant scents like Citrus and Lemon Grass, she invented a product to cater to the increase in luxury cleaning products—lavender dryer sheets. Renee fashioned them out of dried lavender seeds and empty tea bags she buys wholesale and sells a package of four dryer sheets for $4.00. They have been quite a hit at the Northern California farmers markets she attends.

"Nothing sells like big bundles of lavender," Nina Foster Basye of Mt. Vernon, Washington, says. "Every Saturday I sell out quickly at the local farmer's market." Nina's largest time consumer in her lavender business is weeding her quarter acre garden. "It all looks so lovely out there in the fields, but it needs constant weeding in order to keep the plants growing and healthy." She sells her lavender bunches for between $5 and $10, depending on the size.

Once you have enough lavender growing in your own garden, how do you turn that into cash? There are many products you can make yourself:

- Dried lavender sachets
- Lavender vacuum powder (basic baking soda to which dried lavender has been added)
- Lavender bath products (dried lavender in muslin bags for long, hot soaks)
- Dried lavender wreaths and flower arrangements
- Dried lavender braids with other cooking herbs woven in

Investigate the local farmer's markets thoroughly before entering with a new lavender product, as it is a popular item among flower and herb sellers and there may already be more than one vendor.

For more tips on how to start up a lavender products business, check out *Start Your Own Herb and Herbal Products Business: Your Step-by-Step Guide to Success*, by Rob and Terry Adams (Entrepreneur Press, 2003).

Specialty Pantyhose

Treating herself to a pedicure every third week, Bonnie Glogover didn't look forward to the hassle that went along with removing her pantyhose. More food for thought was nearby as she watched other patrons at the nail salon simply cut their pantyhose off at the foot before getting their pedicures. She felt there had to be a better way. Bonnie asked her father, Stanley Glogover, who is the brainchild of both the maternity bra and nursing bra patents, to help her make a prototype of a convertible toe.

It took some time between invention and entering the market. Bonnie lost time after signing a confidentiality agreement with an invention company from 2001 to 2003, which was unsuccessful. Wanting to protect her idea, Bonnie spoke to the Washington, DC, U.S. Patent Office, learned of a reputable patent attorney in her area, and proceeded to file for a patent.

Patents and Trademarks

Registering a domain doesn't mean you also own the trademark for that domain. Protect yourself by conducting a trademark search prior to registering your domain. Such a search can be conducted at the U.S. Patent and Trademark Office's Trademark Electronic Search System (TESS). You can find out if other companies hold trademarks for your domain name and what classes they're protected under.

According to the USPTO, a trademark or service mark is "a word, phrase, symbol or design, or a combination of words, phrases, symbols, or designs, that identifies and distinguishes the source of the goods of one party from those of others." A servicemark is the same thing as a trademark, except it "identifies and distinguishes the source of a service rather than a product."

A common misconception about a trademark is that it is all-encompassing. Trademarks and servicemarks are filed under a specific class or classes. There are 45 classes to choose from when filing for a trademark or servicemark. Companies can file under one class or multiple classes depending on the nature of their product or service. A complete list of eligible classes can be found at the "International Schedule of Classes of Goods and Services" at the USPTO web site.

During the patent pending stages in 2003, Bonnie contracted with a top hosiery mill manufacturer to sew the first round. Finally she was able to achieve her dream of creating a high quality Control Top Sheer Pantyhose that is designed to be worn in every season. Versatility is what makes Glogover Hosiery the most unique pantyhose in the world. They can be worn with sandals, and the flap folds back to show off your toes, or wear closed as a traditional hose. And, of course, they make getting a pedicure simple!

Bonnie takes pride in manufacturing her own pantyhose. She says "it's a creative, affordable solution that fills a niche ignored by the major hosiery manufacturers. I dared to be different and take risks and I brought a one-of-a-kind product to market worldwide." You can see Bonnie's creation on her web site at www.glogoverhosiery.com.

Maternity Clothes Designer

Rita Scott's striking, upscale maternity clothing has caught the eye of A-list celebs. They have been worn by stars such as Geena Davis, Courtney Cox, Heidi Klum, and Tracy Gold, to name a few.

Rita Scott was so committed to turning her passion into a business, she enrolled at a prestigious design school while working at her full-time job. Still juggling her day job, she is the owner and designer of Double Occupancy Maternity Fashions, a Carson, California-based company (www.doubleoccupancy maternity.com). Rita manufactures and distributes fashionable, adjustable maternity clothing. All of her styles will fit through all three trimesters of a woman's pregnancy. The line includes casual, business, and evening wear, with prices ranging from $50 to $120.

Rita has been an aerospace quality engineer for 25 years, a very demanding job that includes process improvements, cost savings, and she coordinates all of the task-specific training for new, college grad, Quality Engineers. She admits that she has always worked in this business because it pays so well, but the thought of doing what she loves to do and earning a living is why Rita started her line of clothing.

Rita's $10,000 investment got her up and running, and she started making money right away. She says "Women will always need maternity clothing, and the fashion business has low barriers to entry. In this business you are only limited by your creativity. That includes fashionable designs and innovative business thinking, such as customer-focused marketing."

Her secret weapons have been attending the Fashion Institute of Merchandising and Design (FIDM) in Los Angeles and getting the best training possible, hiring an industry expert as a consultant, and an attorney who specializes in fashion. The most effective marketing for Rita's company has been hiring a full-time sales rep to make phone calls just for her clothing line because the sales reps in the garment mart don't make calls for individual lines, rather, they are trying to sell the whole showroom.

Cell Phone Accessories

Leslie Jordan was tired of losing her cell phone somewhere inside her purse. And then she saw a woman carrying exactly what she needed—a little tiny silk envelope with a long string that fit a phone perfectly. It could be worn around the neck and never lost again; and would be right there when it rang or a call needed to be made. Perfect. Except that Leslie couldn't find one to buy.

"So I got online and hunted everywhere in cyberspace until I found a source. And when I found a source, I decided to go into business for myself." Leslie founded Cell Cache (pronounced "ca-shay") and began to wear her cell phone purse everywhere in order to generate interest and orders. Just walking around with a Cell Cache purse swinging at her side is enough to draw interested people who are likely to buy. "But you have to have a web site to send them to. If you don't make a sale right then and there, if someone says "Well, I'll think about it . . .," if you don't have a web site for her to go to to make the purchase, you have lost the sale," Leslie warns.

Her web site, www.cellcache.com, not only generates orders for the cell phone purses (which also fit an iPod mini perfectly, too!), but also helps her find people who want to buy wholesale. Leslie is happy to sell her products wholesale; you could be the person in your community who walks around wearing a cell phone purse and generating questions about where they can buy one . . . from you!

One of Leslie's best sales methods is recruiting teenaged girls to sell the pretty mini silk purses. "I sold a large batch to one girl who took them to school and sold them to her friends in one day!"

Always keep your eyes peeled for the trends around you and try to think of a way that you too can profit from them. Whether it is cashing in on the craze for cell phones and iPods, or producing trendy car accessories, staying on top of things will always help you find a way to profit in your spare time.

Foraging

It has happened to all dedicated crafters—suddenly they realize that their hobby is expensive! That the cost to buy materials—even at wholesale—will result in a finished product priced way beyond the market. But imagine this . . . what if your materials were *free*?

To become a good forager, you must look at the world in a whole different way; money may be lying at your feet. Look around at what grows in your area—wild greens, blackberries, hanging moss, rocks. Yes, you read that right, rocks.

Like our pioneering ancestors before us, it is still possible to forage in the wild. Sometimes the wild is in your own backyard, sometimes it is in a friendly neighbor's, but no matter where you live there are things growing near you that can be picked for free and sold for terrific profit, or else used as an element in a craft project. What gets foraged nowadays? How about pine cones? A decade ago the lumber industry slumped and loggers went out into the forest to forage for pine cones which fetched a hefty price in Japan. Jennifer has picked flowers and leaves by the side of the road, small pinecones in the forest, and lichen (or goat's beard) that she fashioned in to holiday wreathes for sale.

Among the things that can be foraged in the wild are: acorns, mistletoe, moss and lichen, wild mushrooms, berries, wildflowers, autumn leaves, evergreen branches and boughs, eucalyptus, pine cones of all sizes, thistles and teasels, fallen wood, dried grasses, pussy willows, wild roses, wild herbs, heather, holly, manzanita, rocks and pebbles, seedpods, cattails, wheat, pine needles, owl pellets, and mugwort.

When foraging in the wild there are several things to keep in mind. The first and most important is to research your finds. Always know what you have collected and whether it is safe. Wild mushrooms should never be collected and sold for food unless you have learned the field thoroughly; some are extremely poisonous, so mushrooming is not for amateurs. The other thing to keep in mind is that while so much of what grows in nature seems like it should be available for us to take without question, it is not. Be sensitive to private property and always get permission from the owner. It is illegal to remove anything from a national park or forest. Keep these rules in mind.

Stern warnings aside, start to look at the world in a whole new way. What you need to make a marketable product might literally be right at your feet!

Sanitary Nailkits

Dr. Carolyn Siegal, a well-respected podiatrist with a thriving practice in Beverly Hills, knew she needed to be proactive when she began noticing her patients had an alarming increase of diseases like fungal infections and plantar warts. Apprehensive and concerned, she started taking her own personal manicure implements to nail appointments and advised her patients to do the same. Her goal was to help people get their nails done without having to worry about the dangers of infections.

Getting prepared to follow the doctor's instructions was easier said than done—Dr. Siegal's patients couldn't find all the recommended tools, and they didn't know how to carry them. It wasn't long before Dr. Siegal's mind started mapping out a plan and building a business around the need in the marketplace. She purchased the implements from a local supplier, hired a seamstress, and got her sister's babysitter to assemble the fashionable little tote bags to carry them in.

Soon her clients wanted to buy several nail kits at a time so they could give them to loved ones like their mothers, daughters, sisters, or friends. Already selling at least 40 kits a week, Dr. Siegal knew she found her niche and began looking for ways to take her idea to the next level.

Her immediate concern was to find vendors who had quality implements and better prices if she was going to sell more nailkits. With the business taking off so quickly, Dr. Siegal knew it was time to hire a seasoned pro to do her business plan. At this point, her husband became her first investor. When he gave her $20,000 for the business he told her, "This isn't a gift, it's an investment."

Next, her sister and her sister's husband joined the family business. They started meeting regularly and the company took on a unique family dynamic. Each one of them possessed qualities that offered a lot to the company: Her sister is an attorney and knows about accounting, her brother in-law is a web designer. Dr. Siegal's own husband is a vascular surgeon. He serves as the strategic advisor.

When it came time to grow the business, Dr. Siegal needed to accomplish two things: outsourcing the production of her implements overseas (the minimum order was 50,000) and start calling stores to get orders for her nailkit. And she had to overcome the uneasiness she felt about knocking on doors to see if people were interested in her product.

Realizing that her nailkit was not only useful, it was also fashionable and a good match for clothing boutiques and would fit nicely with the gift market, she was energized about her prospects. And during the Christmas holiday, Saks Fifth Avenue came on board and went through three orders in two months.

It wasn't until Dr. Siegal participated in the Los Angeles Gift Show that she struck gold by securing 80 new accounts, which gave her orders totaling 25,000 nailkits. She has discovered that educating the public using word-of-mouth to promote her product and having a good public relations person who knows how to appeal to major magazines and TV shows are two powerful tools that helped her business succeed.

In the summer of 2005, her part-time business hit the publicity jackpot—mentions in both Oprah's magazine, "O," and *inStyle* magazine. Check out her kits at www.clshealthyfeet.com.

Special Occasion Sign Rentals

Birthdays, anniversaries, weddings, job promotions, births, and all manner of other noteworthy occasions can be celebrated in high style with a "special occasion sign" planted on the recipient's lawn. You've seen them, the gravestone that mockingly commemorates a fortieth birthday or the happy stork bearing news of a new baby.

Part-time entrepreneur Dean Handy rents his Yard Cards to folks who wanted a high-profile celebration. "With the birth announcements, it is usually the dad who orders the sign. Fortieth birthdays and the like, it is bound to be either the wife or a couple of friends playing a trick." Dean created an inventory of 30 signs for all occasions and rents them for one day, three days, or an entire week. The cost included delivery, installation, and pick up. Dean handmade all of the signs based on drawings he hired an artists to do for him. He blew up the designs and then traced them onto wood, cut them out with a jigsaw, and hand painted the signs. Big bunny rabbits for birthdays and birth announcements, a large "Grim Reaper" that is popular for 30th, 40th, 50th birthdays and so on, and a carousel horse, were among his most popular.

Dean is an independent operator, and has stayed away from using large storks as birth announcements as there is a nation-wide sign-rental franchise that specializes in storks, and he felt he needed to offer a different product.

The special occasion sign business is well suited for weekend entrepreneurs. "Most rentals do take place on the weekends," Dean pointed out. "People like to have the signs out front during birthday parties, and that is when they are generally held."

Special occasion signs rent around the country for $55 for a three-day rental, and $65 for a five-day rental. Check out the competition that is already in your area before making a move on this idea. Most mid-sized communities can really only support one of these businesses.

When Dean was first starting out, he worked on his signs in his front yard and attracted a lot of attention and interest from passersby. He also planted his own signs in his yard occasionally, although not so often or so many that he annoyed his neighbors. Make sure to include your phone number on a discreet part of the signs you rent to generate interest and orders from folks who have seen them in use.

Used Book Store

Stephanie Chandler worked in the Silicon Valley during the dot-com boom and through the bust. Her job selling high-end software to some of the biggest clients in the area required her to meet a $4 million quota. This pressure to perform took a silent toll on Stephanie's health.

The idea to open a bookstore came to Stephanie in a flash one night. One Friday night she was at home, exhausted from another long week, and started stewing about what to do about her career. Over the years Stephanie's love for books led her to sell books on Amazon.com and eBay while working in software sales. During this period she was building a 42-page business plan that took a year and a half to complete. By August of 2003 Stephanie signed a lease on a space for her bookstore and quit her job. It took two months to sort and price her starting inventory of 25,000 books and she had to make repairs and spruce the place up before its grand opening in November 2003. The investment was around $30,000. Stephanie hit the break-even point ten months later and has been more profitable every month since.

Book Lovers is not your typical used book store. The store's tag line is "The neat and organized used book store." Customers are always greeted by a smiling face and a friendly cat. Stephanie was very focused on beating her competitors and studied them carefully. There are more than 20 bookstores within a ten-mile radius of her store and most of them are crammed into small locations; Stephanie chose a spacious 2,800 square foot location. The overall atmosphere at Book Lovers is comfortable and cozy, and she plays good music like Frank Sinatra, Steve Tyrell, and Michael Buble.

Direct mail coupons and Stephanie's monthly store newsletter have worked really well to promote Book Lovers as compared to expensive newspaper ads. She has gone against the norm by hosting book signing events and has been featured in local media at least a dozen times.

People are constantly telling Stephanie that their sister/friend/mother/aunt told them about the store. Recently one woman told Stephanie, "I've been telling everyone I know about your store, but they've all already been here!"

Her costs are low because she doesn't spend a lot on inventory; 90 percent of books come from customer trade-ins and when customers use their credit cards toward a book purchase, they have to pay half in cash. This keeps her cash flow up, and it's a win-win for everyone.

One of the ways Stephanie learned the bookselling business was by e-mailing book store owners all over the country (she found their e-mail addresses on the internet) and asked for advice, "about half of them wrote back and gave her some great tips. It just goes to show—never be afraid to ask for the help you seek!" Stephanie's web site, www.bookloverscafe.com also has information for budding entrepreneurs about how to start their own businesses.

Bridal Accessories

Christina Garcia has a passion for fashion and it all started when she was a little girl. During her formative years, while her friends were engrossed with Barbie dolls and running around playing hide-and-go-seek, Christina was preoccupied with stringing beads and creating her own necklaces and bracelets. Things that sparkled like crystal beads and pearls held a special place in her heart.

But like many of us, Christina's love for jewelry took a back-seat when she went to college to pursue "more realistic" goals. She graduated with a degree in Psychology and her plan was to get a Master's Degree in Occupational Therapy. Just before starting graduate school, Christina had a change of heart. She called off her plans to become an occupational therapist, and immersed herself in art and jewelry-making classes that re-ignited her life-long love for jewelry.

Her family and friends quickly became more than fans, they were her first customers. Their praise and support gave Christina the confidence to take her creations to arts-and-crafts shows where she was a huge success. What Christina observed was that most of her customers were brides who were ecstatic because they finally found high-quality bridal jewelry.

With all of this success, in October 2000 she and her husband, Jerry, started Christina Garcia—Tiaras of Distinction and right away magazines like *Town and Country*, *Modern Bride*, and *Martha Stewart Living* took notice and began featuring her bridal headpieces and accessories. You can view her work at www.christinagarciabridal.com.

Christina's husband Jerry recently finished medical school and as a full-time resident doctor he plans to help with the marketing aspects of the business in his spare time. One of the truly unique aspects of Christina's business is that she has traveled extensively around the world in search of precious materials to incorporate into her designs. The pearls she uses come directly from pearl farms in Asia where she handpicks them to ensure the highest quality for brides. She continues to expand her style and technique by learning from artisans from other countries. Christina's on-the-job training that helped make this company a success came from many of the salons that sell her products.

According to Jerry, the business has exceeded his expectations. It was initially conceived as something for Christina to stay busy with while he was in medical school but it has turned into a great business venture with retailers around the country. They have grown from literally making the jewelry in an apartment on their kitchen table in Minneapolis to an operation with numerous suppliers and manufacturers from the United States and around the world.

Handmade Beeswax Candles

Jennifer's greatest love as a weekend entrepreneur is beeswax candles. One five-minute lesson 15 years ago in how to roll the candles and she was hooked. She makes them to give away as hostess gifts, for birthdays and holidays, and as housewarming presents. In the fall she also hits the crafts fair circuit and sells her handmade wares there.

She buys the flat sheets of colored beeswax from a local bee-keeping supply store, Sacramento Beekeeping (916-451-2337) and generally only makes candles in a limited color range. Since most of her sales occur in the fall, she sticks to the Thanksgiving colors of pumpkin, maroon, dark greens, and gold. She also includes red, white, and green colors for early Christmas purchases. Each candle takes only 30 seconds to produce and she can easily spend an evening watching a favorite television show while rolling up enough stock for a weekend crafts fair.

Each individual sheet costs $1.75 (less if you make large purchases and buy in bulk) and can make two six-inch tapers. A pair of tapers can then be sold at a crafts fair or farmers' market for $5, giving you a healthy mark-up! You'll also need to buy wicks but they are inexpensive in large quantities and do not add much to the cost of your supplies.

Learning to make beeswax candles is not difficult. If there is a beekeeping supply store in your community, check to see if they carry candle supplies, and if they teach classes.

In addition to Sacramento Beekeeping Supply, which does a brisk mail order business, sheets of beeswax in many colors may be purchased from www.knorrbeeswax.com.

Designing and Leading Custom Tours

Bruce Kayton has an unusual knowledge about a seldom-seen side of New York City—he knows the history of "radical New York." For a reasonable tour fee he will lead you for several hours by the places where Emma Goldman lived, where Abbie Hoffman hid, and where famous protests and strikes were held. He has led several thousand people from all over the world on his tours since starting the company in the early '90s.

In San Francisco you can take a walking tour of Chinatown that leads you into noodle factories to watch the process and sample the wares. In Los Angeles you can take a night tour of neon signs. Yes, you can drive around and look at famous and not-so-famous neon signs. These quirky tour leaders base their success on their genuine interest and personal knowledge of their subjects and their good fortune to live in cities rife with color, culture, and history. But you don't have to live in a big city to create and lead unusual tours. With a little imagination and a lot of research you can come up with a tour idea that will work in your area.

Leading tours is a perfect weekend business, as that is when tourists come to town looking for something to do. However, this is not a business for shy people, you must feel comfortable speaking in front of groups. A sense of humor doesn't hurt either. Most walking tours should last two to three hours, and tour prices can range from $15 to as much as $50.

There are endless possibilities for tour ideas. Live out in the country? Why not develop a guided tour of "u-pick" farms and lead a group of food-loving folk from farm to farm, berry picking and pea plucking, ending up in a great down-home restaurant? During the fall you can organize tours around beautiful leaves and fall colors. The countryside has history too; research major events and work them into your talks.

What are some of the best topics to organize quirky tours around? Food, history, scenery, and art. All of these topics have devoted fans who like to use travel as a way to indulge in their interests. Gardening and birding also have millions of devotees.

Develop an original and well-researched tour, start by giving it to your friends and family to hone your skills, and then fire up a press release. Not only can you get publicity in your local media, but don't overlook national newspapers looking for quirky stories and travel magazines always on the lookout for local color.

Product Development and Distribution

Brian Eddy was an attorney by day, practicing law at a firm, but his real passion was spending time as the CEO of Q3 Innovations (www.q3i.com), a company that he started with a childhood friend. Q3 Innovations was founded with $100, and now six years later, Eddy has successfully marketed the Alcohawk ABI digital breath alcohol screener to retailers like The Sharper Image and Target. He has also been able to quit his day job as a lawyer!

Brian got the idea while working for a defense attorney who represented clients charged with drunk driving offenses in Iowa City, Iowa, while he was in law school. He couldn't believe how many clients said, "I wouldn't have driven had I known my BAC was that high." After discussing the potential of an affordable personal breathalyzer with his business partner, Chad Ronnebaum, they found a company online that manufactured a disposable alcohol tester.

Together they formed Q3 Innovations in the summer of 1999, but they didn't purchase any inventory until they became a distributor of the disposable testers in December. By January 2000, after purchasing a thousand dollars in inventory, orders started rolling in and they became profitable within the first couple of months.

Passionate about his business, Brian now puts all of his time toward Q3 Innovations without feeling torn about a day job.

Although Brian says a business school provides a solid foundation on which to start and run a business, a law degree doesn't hurt. He was just getting started with law school when the business took off. His law degree and the knowledge gained as a business law attorney while working with several companies has been extremely useful while building a successful company that has generated outstanding sales.

With annual gross revenues exceeding $1,000,000—Q3 Innovations is a product design, development, and distribution company creating innovative products with an emphasis in the personal safety device market. Q3 Innovations is uniquely positioned to take advantage of the rapidly growing safety devices market with the introduction of its Alcohawk™ Series line of personal breath alcohol screeners.

Do you harbor dreams of distributing a hot new product on a large scale? Start by getting specific information in *Start Your Own Wholesale Distribution Business: Your Step-by-Step Guide to Success*, by Bridget McCrea (Entrepreneur Press, 2003) and see where it can take you!

T-Shirt and Clothing Company

Sometimes, weekend entrepreneurs grow their businesses so large that they go worldwide! Gerard Murray is a perfect example of where your spare-time business can take you.

Starting with a dream, no college degree, and without a business plan, Gerard Murray, Founder and CEO of School of Hard Knocks (SOHK, www.Sohkonline.com), started selling T-shirts with inner-city slogans and developed it into a world-class business with $27 million in sales.

In the early 1990s Gerard took his neighborhood in Queens, New York, by storm when he started selling T-shirts. One of his first T-shirt designs had *"Corona,"* the area where he lived on the front, and the back read *"It's a Black thing and you wouldn't understand it."*

While Gerard worked full-time at Delta Airlines he went to nightclubs all over New York City selling and promoting his T-shirts. Using credits cards to help finance his business and even borrowing money from the credit union at his job, he kept his business afloat.

It took about six years of hard work in his free time before his efforts paid off. The long hours and his relentless drive to promote School of Hard Knocks T-shirts created a buzz worldwide. From California to Japan, people were trying to get their hands on his T-shirts but his distribution channels were limited. In 1998 Gerard signed a deal to license School of Hard Knocks clothing and this catapulted his dream to multi-million dollar status.

Where did Gerard's idea come from? He saw a need for these shirts in his own world, realizing that the popular collegiate-type shirts sporting the names of Ivy League schools didn't accurately represent his local community. Having worked in his own father's clothing store and armed with an understanding of the business, Gerard started his own T-shirt company to develop designs that were more relevant to the people around him. He approached it from a grassroots perspective and the community welcomed his creations with open arms. In the beginning, his T-shirts didn't always come out the way he wanted them to (depending on who he hired to print them). So he gave the ones that didn't look good away for free. For three years after starting the business, Gerard kept reinvesting his profits. He quickly expanded his clothing line after securing a lucrative licensing deal. He started with T-shirts and sweatshirts, then added matching caps, then jeans; he says it wasn't long before women started asking for baby doll T-shirts. School of Hard Knocks was the perfect name because Gerard feels it reflects his life experience and the road he and his father traveled. His clothing line is now sold in over 3,000 stores nationwide.

Take a look around your community. Is there a need for similar locally made and distributed T-shirts that involve local slogans, local issues, local personalities? You might well be able to duplicate Gerard's Queens-based idea in your area.

Home and Garden Parties

According to statistics, Sally Lowry, has beaten the odds. Depressing research estimates that seven out of ten American women will retire in poverty. This stark reality is very familiar to Sally, she sees it all around her on a daily basis. It isn't Sally's reality because at 66 years old she earns more than $300,000 a year as a Home and Garden Party rep. Her business was profitable within 90 days and she qualified for the highest level in the company in just 5 months. The daughter of a salesman, Sally's father always told her "you don't get rich working for someone else."

A few years ago Sally didn't have access to the wealth and the vibrant lifestyle she and her husband enjoy today. Now their life is filled with the joy of knowing they are providing college funds for their grandchildren, and their legacy to their children will be this successful business. In the past Sally and her husband had made a few bad decisions, fell on bad times, and lost everything, including their home. Almost overnight, at 58 years old, this woman went from wondering how they were going to make it—at the time they were living with one of their kids—to taking a chance and joining Home and Garden Party.

Why did she choose this particular party plan company? The trust factor was high because one of Sally's business associates was connected with Home and Garden Party. Upon joining, she and her husband enlisted three other ladies to come on board and immediately they began to build their team. The first year, Sally and her husband earned $40,000, the second year $80,000, and by year three they had a six-figure income.

Are you ready for this? Today Sally has 5,500 people on her team and the numbers are steadily increasing. When it comes to sharing her secrets to party plan success, Sally says, "As long as your mouth is open your business is open. It's just a matter of talking to people about your business and finding an opportunity to talk to them about what you are doing." Sally is grateful for the success she has achieved but says there is no magic bullet; she loves what she does but it is hard work. Had she not gained this fame and fortune Sally would be struggling to survive on a monthly Social Security check of approximately $700.

Sound like it might work for you? You can visit Sally's web site at www.HGPFamily.com and learn more about the Home and Garden Party opportunity at their corporate web site, www.homeandgardenparty.com.

Designer Aprons

Who would have thought the humble apron—once scorned as a symbol of a woman's life of drudgery—would ever make a comeback? According to *The Wall Street Journal*, aprons are "enjoying a renaissance as a retro-chic fashion accessory." The stylish new aprons average around $35 but climb as high as $200, and are referred to as "luxury utilitarian."

College co-eds Flannery E. M. Good and Amy Angeli Durham met during a semester abroad in London. They graduated and took similar career paths, both pursuing careers working for large corporations. However, eventually they became disenchanted with working nine-to-five and decided to combine their creative talents in a business venture. In 2004 they launched their limited edition designer apron collection. You can view their creations at www.flanneryandangeli.com.

Flannery's mother was the inspiration for the business. She used designer home furnishing fabrics left over from her interior design days and made a very stylish apron for Flannery when she got her first apartment. Flannery did a lot of research and found there wasn't anything like her apron on the market. Flannery and Amy became business partners and their first step was to rent a booth at a retail trade show in Sacramento, California. The response was overwhelmingly positive.

With the help of Flannery's mother, these two young women were ready to react to the lack of quality aprons that were available in the marketplace. Most aprons they found were poorly made and used cheap drab fabrics. They set out to change that. Flannery's mother designed the first aprons using leftover home furnishing fabrics. This allowed them to launch a designer apron collection that proved to be both practical and chic.

The resources that the duo found most helpful were the Small Business Administration, SBDC, Central Valley Business Incubator's Accelerator Online course, Entrepreneur's *Start Your Own Business* by Rieva Lesonsky (2004), and the encouragement of their friends and families.

For those wanting to duplicate this type of business, the two recommend adult education classes on designing and creating a web site; they used their own houses as the backdrop for photos and they even modeled their aprons for their photo shoots.

For their public relations campaign, they found a way to get the word out without spending a lot of money on marketing by creating an online site, so didn't have to invest any money in a physical retail space. Flannery says they truly believe that in order to start a business it takes a little bit of money, a good idea, and a lot of determination.

In an effort to keep their business thriving, Flannery and Amy both have day jobs but work on their apron business every chance they get. They operate an online retail site selling their stylish, high-end aprons. They select the fabrics, design the aprons, and have them manufactured. They sell all over the United States via their web site, which they created and maintain. Their tenacity in marketing to magazine editors and their high quality product has landed them on the pages of several publications.

Considering the relatively small amount of time and money—they have invested just $2,000 in this venture—they have become quite a success. Keeping an eye on the latest trends in fashion, Flannery and Angeli aprons are intentionally made in small quantities to ensure their uniqueness in the market place. Right now they earn about $1,000 a month selling their designer aprons, and each spends five to ten hours a week growing the business and filling orders.

Wedding MC Services

Public speaking skills come in handy at weddings, but so few of us really seem to have the skill! Large weddings need someone to not only speak to the crowd and keep the ball rolling, but also to increase the energy level. So, Pete Miller wondered, why not develop a service around this very real need? And his business, WeddingMC, was born. He supplies a first-class, polished, and professional emcee who knows how to work a crowd.

Where does Pete find the folks who can handle this kind of pressure and spotlight, to walk into a large situation and keep it all running? Actors and experienced television presenters are his best emcees. Speaking more than one language is also a plus for his presenters.

There is a big difference between DJing and MCing, Pete likes to point out. "Our only real competitors are DJs who convince the bride and groom that they can save the couple money by MCing and DJing at the same time—when in fact, the MCing they perform is very substandard, by virtue of the fact that they are stuck behind a console. Unfortunately, the unlucky couple only discover this during their wedding reception and not before."

Pete's business grew out of the fact that he himself is an actor, and always in need of income between acting jobs. Once he discovered a need for the service, he began to hire other acting friends to help out. And was it profitable? "Immediately. I already had a computer. An MC requires very little capital to start. All we need is a pen, a folder, and a dinner suit. Some MCs carry their own personal PA systems."

His biggest expense has been the web site, www.wedding mc.com.au. "This cost me around four thousand dollars, but it immediately paid for itself." Because of our great web site, the whole process is automated. I interview with the couple a few days before the event to learn more about who they are, what kinds of guests will be there, and what kind of a mood they want to maintain. The wedding reception itself is usually about a six-hour event. The best MCs keep guests entertained and the event organized and running smoothly while always keeping the center of attention on the bride and groom.

How do the happy couple learn about Pete's service? He attends Bridal Expos as a guest (not as an exhibitor) and talks to wedding venue managers at hotels and gardens. He also advertises on local wedding web sites that cater to his area and in a local bridal magazine. Pete's MCs fee is $650 per event. Out of that he keeps $200 as the booking fee, and the rest of the money goes to the MC.

Not a bad bit of change, eh? Do you have what it takes to be an MC? Do you have strong public speaking skills? Are you at ease in front of a crowd of strangers? You could also develop a business that books others as MCs. This is not a business for everyone, but if you'd like to learn more visit Pete's web site, www.weddingmc.com.au. If you'd like to try to develop a similar business in your area, Pete has written a booklet called *You Can Be a Wedding MC* that is available through his web site.

Club and Concert Promotion

Dennis Anderson loves going to concerts, seeing the behind the scenes of how it all comes together and watching everyone have fun. It was that love and the success of selling his first concert out in 20 minutes that convinced Dennis to make a go of his dream business.

By day he works at a bank. Evenings and weekends are divided between his personal life and running his independent event promotion company, VMG LIVE, Inc. (www.vm glive.com). Dennis also has a family and a full-time job so he has to carefully manage the ten additional hours his concert promotion business demands. He has been promoting concerts on a small scale since August 2001, and his $1,500 marketing budget was enough to get him started.

For Dennis, this has been a learn-while-you-earn business since he hasn't found a lot of books on how to start a promotion company. He found the internet, search engines, and music books dealing with marketing to be helpful. Also, industry magazines such as *Billboard* provide valuable information and resources for Dennis' business.

Although this industry is very competitive, Dennis says there is always room for new companies to emerge. "Everyone wants to see a great event at a great price. If there is a promoter that is willing to provide great entertainment and has a strong knack for marketing, he or she will do well." Dennis is still building his business but says that on a small scale, the average income is approximately $35,000 a year. However, if you are promoting at arenas, you can do well over $300,000 a year. Dennis is quick to admit that the business hasn't been easy, but sticking to it has helped him on the road to achieving everything he has ever wanted in a business.

Do you have a knack for getting publicity and building a crowd? Then part-time concert promotion might be for you. Start investigating the market in your area by talking to club owners and bands, find out if there is a need and ask them how best you could fill it.

Let's Check Your Progress

Did any of these 30 ideas grab your imagination? Can you see yourself leading tours of the historic graveyards in your area, growing lavender to make into products for a farmers' market stand on the weekends, or perhaps developing a business as a professional master of ceremonies for weddings? Is there maybe a part of one of these ideas that you might be able to reshape to better suit your own talents or the community in which you live? You might want to let some of these ideas percolate in your brain for a bit before moving on to the next batch of weekend entrepreneur-worthy pursuits.

After you've mulled these ideas over, you'll be ready for the next batch of businesses. Turn on your laptop, as these are all online and computer-based.

5

BOOT IT UP
Making Extra Money with Online Businesses and Internet Auctions

So many promises were made about the computer age—that it would save us all time, that it would save us all paper. So far it hasn't really done much of either of those, but there was an unexpected benefit—who knew that it could make us all money?

Among the best part-time and weekend entrepreneurial opportunities are businesses that happen online. Instead of standing behind the stall at your local farmers' market waiting for the bundles of lavender to sell, instead of physically being anywhere at any specific time, an online business is ideally suited to working when and where you can.

In this chapter, we've identified 25 different types of businesses that can be started and operated in your spare time with your computer. Many of these started out spare time and then morphed in to full-time pursuits. We hope these online businesses open your eyes to the myriad of ways to make money with your computer and an online connection.

Travel Business

When Laura Johnson's husband was unexpectedly laid off from a very good job, money was tight and they didn't know how they were going to make their next mortgage payment. Laura recalls, "I needed to do something to help bring in some income. Our daughter was just eight months old, so I was looking for something I could do from home to bring in the money we needed." So when Laura heard about a way to earn money while taking vacations at wholesale prices, she was very excited. She felt this might be a way to change their lives for the better.

This sounded like a perfect fit because both Laura and her husband always loved to travel; every year they would save their money and go on a nice trip for their anniversary. Laura signed on in the Associate Travel Agent Program with Global Travel Trends, the fastest growing online travel agency in the world. She now enjoys large discounts on travel and makes money working from home. The business was a success right away and Laura said, "After three months of working part time, I was earning more than my husband made full time, so we decided it was a good time for us both do the business."

They started out working about 10 hours each a week, but soon they were putting in close to 30 hours a week. However,

Laura loves it because "it is so much fun, it is hard to say exactly where fun stops and work begins because part of our working hours are out doing things we enjoy, and talking to people." The most effective way they have found to market this business opportunity is through word of mouth, having what they call "Travel Parties" and "Travel Orientations."

Global Travel Trends has over 160,000 associate travel agents worldwide in over 65 countries and one of the best compensation plans in the travel industry. Associates can take five-star vacations for one- and two-star prices. Becoming a credentialed Associate Travel Agent allows people to earn commissions from any travel booked off of their exclusive web site (which is partnered with Travelocity, Hotwire, Orbitz, Expedia, etc.). They also earn a tremendous amount of money through introducing people to the company so they can also travel at wholesale prices by becoming their own travel agent.

Does this sound like a part-time business you would enjoy? Mixing travel and an income is the dream of many. Global Travel Trends does have a business opportunity available for dedicated travelers who'd like to make money from their love for travel. Check it out at www.time2go.gttrends.net.

Electronic Hookup Specialist

Although the businesses in this chapter are largely centered on making money online, what about making money by helping other people *get* online? Or even get their stereo working? Or that new fancy TV that requires special knowledge to hitch up? Jennifer's husband, Peter, has performed this function for years for the older folks around him; he is the "go-to" guy whenever anyone has a new high-tech gadget. New stereos, computers, digital cameras, home theaters, you name it, and someone out there can't figure out the directions and needs to hire someone else to set it up.

Is that a knack you already possess? Then it is high time to start advertising your skills and charging a professional price— $30 an hour—for your help.

Think of a clever name for yourself (Geek Squad is already taken!). We'd recommend staying away from any pun on "hooking up" as it has sexual connotations that won't appeal to the older audience that needs you the most. Make up a flier, get the word out, and start plugging in all those confusing wires for folks!

A less technical alternative would be to advertise your skills as an assembler. Set up furniture, put together a bicycle, almost anything from a retail store that comes in a box needs to be assembled. You'd be surprised at how often customers are intimidated by what they buy once they get it home!

Virtual Assistant

In Santa Cruz, California, Mahesh Grossman of AuthorsTeam .com is a businessman on the move, and needed an assistant who could move with him. Sort of. Charlene Turner lives in Utica, New York, and she follows him everywhere. Sort of. Charlene is a freelance virtual assistant, who does work for a number of entrepreneurs scattered across the country. She worked for one client, Andrew Morrison of Small Business Camp for two full years before she finally met him!

Charlene was working full time as a human resources professional on Wall Street when she met an entrepreneur in desperate need of organizational help. "I offered to help him get his business organized for free, just because I was curious about his business." That led to a paid part-time gig when he recommended her to another associate. "And that man needed help with a web site and basic graphic design. Not things I knew about but my attitude was such that I thought hey, I'll go out and learn." And learn she did. She learned so much and did such a good job that he recommended her to one of his friends, who recommended her to another, and, well, you get the idea.

With a steady income from a client base located around the country, Charlene was able to leave the stress of New York City and Wall Street behind and move upstate. Her base rate is $17 an hour. "Some virtual assistants charge $25 an hour, but I noticed that they work a lot less than I do, so I keep my rates reasonable." Many of her clients are business success coaches, and she has found that her clients are her best marketers—"nine out of ten clients are referrals. Word of mouth gets me a lot of business."

What kinds of assistance is Charlene able to provide when she isn't physically working in someone's office? Take a look at this list.

- Word processing
- Desktop publishing and corporate newsletters
- Human resources functions
- Database management
- Sales and marketing support
- Web design and development
- Audio recording and editing
- Employee data management

Do you have what it takes to be a virtual assistant? You need to have solid basic secretarial skills like typing and notetaking, and be adventurous and willing to learn new things. Much of what Charlene now does she had to go out and learn once someone asked her to help them with it! "With each project I learn so much, sometimes I feel like I'm getting paid to learn," Charlene says. If that sounds like a part-time business you would enjoy, Charlene also offers one other service—you can hire her as a consultant to teach you how to successfully operate a virtual assistant business! Take a look at her web site at www.vpsworks.com.

Online Community

There have been several successful examples of enterprising folks creating online communities that ultimately generated income for them. It isn't a guaranteed thing, but if you find the right niche, create the right community, and strike the right chord with the folks in your community, you can build traffic to the point where you will be able to create revenue streams.

Whatever are we talking about? Online communities. The most successful one of all is Craigslist, which grew out of an informal e-mail alert a guy named Craig Newmark in San Francisco began to send to his friends in the mid-90s. Craig mostly wanted to tell his friends about cool parties that were happening. Then he began to let them add in information they had about job openings, vacant apartments, stuff for sale, and so on. The list grew and grew and grew and is now in most major cities in the United States. Craigslist didn't start out to make money but it certainly does—by selling online classified ads to employers (all other types of ads are free to craigslist users).

Mary Goulet and Heather Reider saw a need for an online community that catered to stay-at-home moms. Hello Moms Town! (www.momstown.com) now includes an internet radio show, chat boards to exchange information, helpful free articles on a number of topics, and lots of information for moms who want to start work-from-home businesses. How do Mary and Heather make money from their community? Within three months of starting their online community, they caught the eye of a book editor and landed a hefty publishing contract! They also put on seminars, charging $95 for a two-day workshop on starting a business from home. Their web site now ranks in the top 10,000 of most visited sites!

Several other success stories come to mind—Michael Cader, a book packager, started a free ezine to send to others in the industry with publishing news and gossip. He called it Publishers Lunch. His newsletter now reaches some 15,000 professionals in that industry and has spawned a busy web site, Publishers Marketplace, that charges a monthly membership fee. Laurel Touby started Media Bistro to connect magazine publishing professionals; it has now spawned a large multi-city organization that mounts seminars, has online classes and courses, and puts on networking parties.

Do you have an interest, professional or personal, that might signal the existence of an undiscovered community? Perhaps you can build a community around one of your hobbies—building bird houses, for instance, or needlepointing. Begin with a newsletter that you send to the other enthusiasts you know, and ask them to send it on to their friends as well. All successful online communities start with a small idea and a small group of folks and spread out from there.

How do you make money? Like Momstown, you can ultimately create classes, seminars, or organized get-togethers where dedicated members of the community come together face to face. Once your traffic grows, you can begin to approach sponsors and advertisers who want to reach your audience. And like Publishers Marketplace and Media Bistro, you can create a paid membership that allows members into special sections of the web site with additional valuable professional information.

Memory Boxes

Gift baskets have been around for the past few decades as a business idea, and hardly ever seem new and fresh. But two enterprising women have discovered an online niche and made it work for them! Just like some of the craft businesses you read about in Chapter 4, Mona Mensing and Nancy Cunningham have taken their own interests and inspiration and developed a product. But instead of sitting at a craft fair waiting for customers to stroll by, they leapt online to look for sales!

Gift baskets found in stores have traditionally been already designed and ready to go, such as a baby shower gift basket filled with basic necessities an expectant mom would want. But picture a vintage suitcase filled with an old 45 record from the 1950s in which a slick-haired singer longs for his "baby," an old-fashioned patterned bib, and hand lotions and soaps with an antique look to them. Sounds like more fun than what you'd buy off the shelf as a gift!

Instead of a cookie cutter approach, each of the baskets that Polk-a-dot Packages produces is individually designed with the recipient in mind. These two women have put a fresh spin on an old idea and developed a following online for their clever gift offerings. You can see their offerings on www.polkadotpack ages.com.

Check out the "themed baskets" section on eBay and let your imagination soar about what kinds of themes you could produce!

Janestones

Sacramento artist Jane Goldman sells her paintings and jewelry regularly at local galleries and shows. But instead of just limiting herself to the folks who can come and see her work in person, Jane has developed an online presence to market her work.

Jane actually prefers to sell her work online rather than to sit at a craft show booth and watch disinterested folks walk by. "It is hard to see someone walk by without looking, and it is even harder when they come to your booth, pick up your work, try it on, and then put it down and walk away. And can you imagine what it is like to hear someone discuss your work like you aren't even there?

In addition to her chunky stone bracelets, earrings, and necklaces, Jane has added an additional product—handpainted canes. Jane uses a cane herself after a gardening accident (yes, a gardening accident!) and was frustrated by how dull and stodgy the basic cane looked. So she painted one for herself and every time she goes out into public with it she is approached by someone who wants to buy one for herself, her mother, or an elderly friend. Talk about street marketing! You can see her work at www.janestones.com.

"Don't listen to people who say you should never make your hobby into a business because then it won't be fun. They're so wrong! It's even more fun. I get such a good feeling when I see someone wearing one of my pieces, what could be more fun than that?"

Do you have a handcraft that you are reluctant to try to sell yourself in person? Building an online site might be the answer. How do you build traffic to your site, though? Send press releases to magazines and newspapers with photos of your work and information about your web site, create parts of your web site that have information for other people interested in the same hobby, and be sure to send out a link to all of your friends and family!

Gourmet Coffee Cakes and More

When it comes to multi-tasking, Sherry Comes has mastered the art of getting things done at lightening speed, and she has a successful e-commerce business to prove it. A *Wall Street Journal* secret shopper rated CoffeeCakes.com "Best Overall" because the storefront was "well-organized and easy to navigate." Sherry holds down a full-time job as an executive IT architect for a major company, and in her spare time she is president of CoffeeCakes.com, a Colorado-based web site.

Getting up as early as 4 A.M. permits Sherry to manage her gourmet food and gift business. She says "I am the best delegater; I totally run my business on relationships." By simply outsourcing both her call center and fulfillment operation, the business doesn't need employees to run smoothly. However, Sherry took great pride in building her web site's platform, which she personally coded, otherwise it would have cost around $100,000. "As a very senior professional in designing [software] architecture for Fortune 500 companies, I have built an infrastructure that could scale to a million orders a day," she says.

CoffeeCakes.com is the brainchild of an unsuccessful bricks-and-mortar coffee shop Sherry started in 1995. After customers kept wanting to know how to send Sherry's delicious gourmet coffee cakes and gifts to friends and family around the world, she finally took note and started growing the online storefront CoffeeCakes.com as a gourmet gift site. By 2000 it was a 100 percent online internet retailer.

This company is funded, owned, and operated by women. Two of the partners actively participate in the business (the others are investors). Because of her desire to give back to others who may be less fortunate, Sherry has formed a partnership with Erin Brochovich and Cancer411.org where a percentage of all proceeds are donated to cancer research to help cancer patients and their friends and family members.

During the past ten years, CoffeeCakes.com has grown primarily by word of mouth and repeat business. Over half of its orders are repeat customers and Sherry has seen tremendous growth year after year. In 2004, business doubled thanks to very strong repeat business. Her secret weapon is investing a significant amount of time and money in search engine optimization. CoffeeCakes.com was the top paid result in a recent Google search.

How can you cook up a profit online? In order to sell food, you must use a commercial kitchen (one that meets very strict health department standards). Not everyone can afford to build his own commercial kitchen, so look into leasing time at one already in existence—a local restaurant owner, for instance, or your own church might have a commercial kitchen that meets the standard. If you are well-known in your circle for your famous cookies, cakes, pies, or other food that can stand up to being shipped, get into the kitchen and fire it up.

Online Business and Success Coaching

The business of success coaching is exploding everywhere, including online! Your erstwhile authors, Michelle and Jennifer, both recently added "coach" to their own basket of skills.

Michelle's clients come to her with a specific purpose, they want to do a better job on television. You might well have heard Michelle Anton's name over the years—for five years she was the producer of the Dr. Laura radio show. Before that she was a freelance associate producer working on programs suchs as *The Oprah Winfrey Show* and television producer for *Leeza Gibbons* to the *A&E Biography* series. Michelle knows a thing or two about television and radio, and coaches aspiring guests on ways to improve their media strategies and how to be sought-after guests.

Michelle doesn't just limit her coaching to how her clients can look, act, and sound better on camera or over the airwaves; she also points them towards ways to monetize their media appearances. What is the point of appearing on TV to promote a book or web site if, when folks go to your web site, you don't actually have anything to sell them?

Jennifer coaches writers to successfully hone their ideas and projects for the publishing world, and also helps writers with their biggest stumbling block of all—actually finishing the project. "I always warn writers that I am expensive, and I am mean! Expensive to hire, and mean when it comes to relentlessly pushing them to finish their projects. Funny thing, it hasn't discouraged anyone from hiring me! One client even said 'mean! Ooo, I love mean!'"

Jennifer spends several hours each week e-mailing back and forth with encouraging words, specific suggestions, and actual assignments for her clients to follow. Working through e-mail online gives both Jennifer and her coaching clients the chance to communicate at times that work for them. Several of Jennifer's writing clients have worked full time and pursued writing on the side, so e-mail has taken the place of late-night coaching calls. A publishing professional with 25 years of experience and a wide network of contacts, Jennifer's online coaching doesn't come cheap—$75 an hour with a four-hour minimum commitment.

Even online personal trainers for fitness and weight loss are starting to emerge. Accountability is key here, and whether the person you are held accountable to is standing in front of you, a voice on the phone, or comes in an encouraging e-mail, the effect is the same! Setting goals, sticking to the goals, and maintaining contact are what count.

What does it take to build a business online as a success coach? This type of business works best for those who have built substantial records of success themselves. Before you can help someone else succeed, they will expect you to have achieved success yourself. Are you a top leader or producer in your full-time field? Do colleagues and customers often come to you for advice and instruction? You might be well positioned to build a side business as a coach.

Like the virtual assistant business, coaching work can come your way largely by referral once your clients begin to succeed. The better they do, the more they will attribute their success to you and recommend you to others!

eBay Trading Assistant

Everyone is making money on eBay, aren't they? And some people are making money on eBay selling other people's stuff!

Selling on eBay allows you to use a skill you already have and generate income using that skill. It is up to you to negotiate with your client as to what fee or percentage you will charge them. Do this in advance, of course, before you begin working with a client. Make sure you all agree on how much you will be listing the item for, how it will be described, and how long the auction will last. Decide on a minimum fee that you would like to earn—and remember that, as the official seller of the item, eBay will be charging you the seller's fee, so make sure your charge accounts for that too!

How will clients find you? Easy, through the eBay site itself! eBay has developed a Trading Assistant's Directory that customers can access right on the official eBay web site. If someone in your community has an item that he wants to sell on eBay, but doesn't know how and wants someone to do it, he simply types in the zip code and *voila*! eBay does the work!

eBay also supplies you with downloadable promotional materials like posters and signs that you can use to advertise your service around your own community.

You can also limit your services to certain types of items. Perhaps you just want to help sell clothes (which are easy to pack and ship) and not deal with porcelain or china (which is not easy to pack and ship). All you need to do is include your specialties on your eBay Trading Assistant profile.

The requirements are as follows—you must have sold at least four items in the last 30 days; you must have a feedback score of 50 percent or higher; 97 percent of your feedback must be positive; and your eBay account must be in good standing. Is that you? If so, read on.

To stay active in the Trading Assistant's Directory, you must meet those same requirements every month. At the present time it does not cost anything to be listed in the Trading Assistant's Directory on the eBay site, but they warn that it might well be changed in the future.

Personalized Children's Books

How's this for a large market—there are 36 million American children under the age of eight. Wouldn't they all like to own a book that not only had their favorite characters in it, but incorporated their own names and personal information too? Imagine reading the story of a major Disney character like *The Little Mermaid* and seeing your own child's name in the book? What a delightful surprise for any child!

Jack and Wendy Kalisher started their company, Best Personalized Books, so that every child could have that feeling of specialness. The proprietary printing system they developed, along with the exclusive licenses they arrange with all the current hot kid's media properties, make for an outstanding gift that delights its intended target.

Are you interested in starting a part-time business that lets you be involved in something as worthy as children's books and literacy? Perhaps producing and selling personalized children's books might be the right fit for you. Check out their web site at www.bestpersonalizedbooks.com for more information about their business.

Pajamas Online

Sleepyheads.com is the brain child of Françoise Shirley. She says "We decided on a fun, whimsical, 'as seen on TV' sleepwear concept because cocooning was *the* trend six years ago. People were spending more time at home then ever before, and society as a whole was becoming much more casual—people were grocery shopping in their PJ bottoms." In addition, Françoise noticed that TV shows like *Ally McBeal* featured their main characters wearing PJs, which drove the demand. Françoise felt she had the right product at the right time, and was selling it through the right medium, as cocooners tended to also be online shoppers.

She created Sleepyheads.com as a comfy, cozy online boutique for hip, trendy PJs and loungewear.

Françoise and her husband worked full time while they started Sleepyheads.com and initially, their philosophy was that this online venture was just going to be a hobby. However, working in their spare time (sometimes until 3:00 A.M.!) made them realize that this side business needed full-time attention. Six months after starting the business, Françoise's husband quit his job to help run Sleepyheads.com.

Another challenge they had was managing their growth. The entire operation ran from their home including office space and warehousing inventory, every closet was stuffed with pajamas, and their entire garage was full.

It wasn't easy having employees work at their house but they wanted to make sure the success of the concept was long-term before they started leasing a warehouse. They started small and expanded slowly, and with the popularity of Sleepyheads.com they have expanded to a 5,500 square-foot warehouse.

While trying to get settled, they had to learn how to manage buying inventory; because manufacturers work with long lead-times, there was a gap between the time they placed their order to the time it was delivered. So they had difficulty keeping up with demand at first. Now that they know what to expect in terms of sales every quarter, it's easier for them to budget and buy.

No neophyte businesswoman, Françoise spent 11 years in marketing, public relations, advertising special event planning, and running her own advertising agency prior to launching Sleepyheads.com. She gained valuable retail experience running and managing her own gift boutique, and her combined experience helped turn her initial investment of $20,000 into a profit center their first year. No wonder these trendy jammies have been featured on *The View*, *Queer Eye for the Straight Guy*, *The*

Bachelor, *The Today Show*, and in giftbags for the Grammys and Oscars.

E-Books and Special Reports

Although electronic books never took over the marketplace in quite the way publishing pundits predicted a few years back, producing and selling ebooks on hot topics can be a great way to make a second income.

Ebooks are basically a file. Nothing fancier than that. A PDF file that you are sending to someone in exchange for money. You have information they want—info on how to build something like a skateboard ramp, for instance. The customer sends you money via a check or money order, credit card number, or a service like PayPal, you send them the file. It is as simple as that.

So why would someone buy an ebook, rather than go to a bookstore or library looking for the information they need? Several reasons. Speed is one. Need to give a eulogy tomorrow at the funeral of a friend? No time to poke around a bookstore, better go online a type in "eulogy." That takes you to a very basic looking web site run by an ebook genius named Tom Antion. He will sell you an ebook on how to give a thoughtful, respectful, and compelling eulogy. And his site sells the eulogy ebook all day, every day, to the tune of several thousand dollars a month. Not a bad business, is it? Tom Antion has figured out several similarly compelling ideas for ebooks on info that people need in a hurry and will buy online. You might not have to speak at a funeral, you might have to give a toast at a wedding! And Tom can sell you an ebook on that topic, too.

These topics work best:

- How to make money
- How to save money

- How to profit from a well-kept secret of some sort
- How to do something better, faster, and more often

Money, secrets, time, are those topics you can work with? What about an e-book called—*Twenty Ways to Feed Your Family on $5* or *Secrets of Cheap Chic Living*.

Are you seeing a pattern here about the kinds of topics that work well? To learn more about ebooks and how to produce them, marketing gurus Joe Vitale and Jim Edwards run www.7dayebook.com. You'll learn everything you need to be up and running quickly with a book of your very own to market.

Unicycle.com

Jennifer and her husband Peter are the authors of *Niche and Get Rich* (Entrepreneur Press, 2003) and, as you might imagine, are always on the lookout for amazing niche business ideas. As sexy as online businesses sound, they are just like any other business with the potential for competitors, the chance that you might lose customers to a big box retailer, or other standard business risks. The better your niche, however, the lesser the risk.

John Drummond of Marietta, Georgia, has carved out such a niche for his family business: unicycles. Unicycles? Yes, those funky one-wheeled contraptions. John rode one when he was in junior high school, and then put it aside in his garage for 20 or so years before taking up the hobby again. He quickly needed to replace his old unicycle and learned that the selection in his town was slim. An online retail business was born.

John, his wife Amy, and their extended family, now run www.unicycle.com, an international business. Although John imagined that he would spend his entire career at IBM and just run his business in his spare time, within the first eight months it grew too big and he left his computer career.

What do you need to succeed in a field like this? Something with a highly devoted group of users—like unicyclists—who need to turn to specialty retailers to get what they need. It needs to be specialized enough that the big box retailers like Target and Wal-Mart aren't going into carrying that item in a big way. You might be able to find one unicycle for sale in the sports department of a big retailer, but you sure as heck will never find a selection of 20 different models that appeal to the high-end enthusiast.

How do you find a niche idea like this? Look around your own life first—is your hobby a specialized one that appeals to a select group of people? Exotic birding perhaps? Look for needs that can't be efficiently fulfilled by traditional methods of retailing.

Celebrity Cosmetics

Jeanne Marie runs a full-time business powdering people's noses. Well, actually, what she does is make people look wonderful on camera. A professional television and media make-up specialist, she has worked on all manner of celebrities, from politicians like Bill Clinton and Arnold Schwarzenegger to top network anchors like the late Peter Jennings.

Jeanne Marie is based in Northern California, and many of her television clients were just passing through the area during media tours. They liked Jeanne's make-up products so much that they wanted them wherever they traveled! In order to meet the demands from such a far-flung clientele, she started a web-based professional make-up store at www.jeanne marie.com.

Her own brand of high-quality on-air makeup can be customized for each client, giving her business a touch that you don't find at the mall make-up store.

In addition to her own unique brand of cosmetics called International Media Cosmetics, Jeanne Marie had many requests for a treatment product that would keep her celebrity clients looking their best at all times. Working with a chemist, she developed the Pumpkin Peel face mask to combat fine lines and wrinkles.

How much time does it take for Jeanne to run her online business in addition to her daily routine of powdering the noses of important people? She is able to deal with orders in the evenings and ship product out the next morning.

Do you also deal with clients that you might not see again? Why not develop a way to keep them as your clients no matter where they are? Make your products available to them again and again regardless of time or place.

New Media Production Company

Right around the time Paca Thomas was about to retire, Liz Dubelman came to him with a concept. It was ironic because at the time he was searching for a source of residual income; work that made money in perpetuity, rather than the current work-for-hire income that he was receiving as a salaried employee as a Sound Effects Designer with Post Production House. He knew he couldn't let this opportunity pass because it was right up his alley and he and Liz are now partners with VidLit™, which went online in September, 2004. This "new media" venture incorporates sound and picture to promote the written word and to encourage people to read books. Here's what they do—promote nonfiction and literary works that, when people e-mail these animated short videos to their friends, helps create higher visibility for the book and increases sales.

Paca says they didn't have any out-of-pocket initial expenses. The business was able to get off the ground with very low over-head, but both Paca and Liz had to put in countless hours of labor to realize their dream.

The business became popular almost immediately and they paid a price that they hadn't anticipated—the flood of online traffic boosted their server costs so high that they were hemorrhaging what little money they made. A significant amount of time was spent stabilizing the situation in order to restore order and profit.

Since VidLit is used as a marketing tool, marketing a marketing tool has been a fascinating experience for Paca and Liz. Fortunately, the publishing industry, their main source of work, is looking for new ways to sell their wares and has been a major supporter. One of the most effective resources they use to promote the idea to the masses is the internet. Paca says, "We were 'discovered' by a few people who told a few others, who told a few 100,000 others. We witnessed a remarkable phenomenon, a global neighborhood talking to each other over the digital backyard fence."

Paca's work in animation sound at Advantage Audio, along with countless other projects for Disney, Universal, Sony, and Dreamworks, has garnered him five Emmy awards and more than a dozen other industry nominations and awards. Check out his current work at www.vidlit.com.

Gags, Gifts, and Magic Tricks

Jeff Ferguson's love of gags and magic first came from a visit to the Magic Shop on Main Street at Disneyland in Anaheim, California. For some reason, the collection of fake flies in ice cubes, whoopee cushions, and cans of nuts that hid spring loaded snakes appealed to his sense of humor. He was hooked for life.

Jeff was prepared to take a chance with a business idea that may have seemed a little goofy to some. However, his background gave him a solid foundation to create a winner. He's been a veteran in the online marketing field since 1995 with Fortune 500 companies such as Hilton Hotels Corporation and Kimberly-Clark.

Started with his $3,000 severance paycheck, The Gag (www.thegag.com) became self-sustaining after six months of operation. The initial investment was recouped during the start of his second fiscal year of operation. When he's not working as an internet marketing consultant for small- to mid-sized businesses, Jeff is running his online store, which provides the best in classic practical jokes and magic tricks for all ages, from a variety of pranks, practical jokes, gag gifts, card and coin tricks, all at reasonable prices.

The idea for The Gag has taken on many forms over the past few years, but it wasn't until Jeff was over halfway through his MBA when he decided to stop dreaming about this site and actually put together a plan of action . . . plus, Jeff needed a topic for a strategy paper. After the paper received an "A" and accolades from his classmates, he took advantage of his unplanned free time caused by a job layoff and started the first version of The Gag, which lasted for almost two years.

The plan evolved over the years as he learned more about the market and his customers; however, according to Jeff, one of the reasons he was profitable so early was due to the fact that he followed his business plan during the early stages of development. The current iteration was launched in April of 2004, just in time for his first television appearance on *Living it Up! With Ali and Jack*, where his Gag-of-the-Month Club was featured in a segment on unique gifts.

Search Engine Optimization (SEO) has been helpful to Jeff's business. He says, "Paid search drove a significant amount of traffic, but most sales came from natural search results. We believe most of our sales success comes from this source."

Writing and Editing Content

Meryl K. Evans has a diverse writing and editing background. She often covers technology, marketing, web design, and writing.

Clients have used her for other topics because of her expert research and detail-oriented skills. Luckily, Meryl was able to start her company without having any financial burdens because she already had a computer and the resources needed to run a successful business.

Originally, she was planning to do web design, but discovered she preferred writing. After a few writing gigs, Meryl slowly kept adding more work and the business was born. She says "I never dreamed of being in business as I don't like the hassle of bookkeeping. But now I am glad I have the business." Until recently, Meryl was working only part time at her day job but she is back to working full time because the company's workload increased. In addition to her fulltime job, she spends 20 to 30 hours a week on her side business.

Her marketing is done by networking and word of mouth. Meryl's determination and superior writing skills keep clients coming back, she says, "Since I'm profoundly deaf, cold calling is out of the question. I also have a web site and newsletters to help with marketing efforts." She attributes her success to friendly service, meeting deadlines on time, and high quality work. You can see Meryl's site at www.meryl.net.

How are your writing and editing skills? You might have the talent and creativity to flourish with an online writing business.

Word-of-Mouth Marketing

Joining your local chamber of commerce or a networking group is a great way to jumpstart your business. The largest networking organization is Business Network International (BNI). This is a business and professional networking organization that offers members the opportunity to share ideas, contacts, and most importantly, referrals.

Vintage Clothing Boutique

Just as there is a devoted audience out there for unicycles, there is an equally devoted audience for crinoline skirts, or old fur coats, or 1920s flapper dresses. Collectors, hobbyists, fashionistas, and designers are all mad for vintage clothes! Vintage is a catch-all phrase that covers any clothing that isn't up-to-the-minute current. A vintage dress might be from the 1920s, or it might be from the 1980s! Either way, it has a collector out there who would love to add it to her closet.

The online vintage clothing community is large and active. Many sellers confine themselves to eBay, and others build elaborate sites to attract devoted customers. If clothes are your thing, this could be a way to turn your hobby into a money-making business.

Good books on the topic are *Virtual Vintage: The Insider's Guide to Buying and Selling Fashion Online* by Linda Lindroth and Deborah Tornello (Random House, 2002), and *The Official Price Guide to Vintage Fashion and Fabrics* by Pamela Smith (House of Collectibles, 2001).

Where can you find vintage clothes to market? Almost everywhere! Garage sales and estate sales, antique stores and thrift shops, and even your family attic! Use the price guides and information you can glean online about where to start the bidding and let it go up from there!

Niche Music Sales

Not long ago you read about Charlene Turner, virtual assistant extraordinaire. But wait, that isn't the only part-time business she runs! No . . . Charlene's own musical interests led her to develop an online site that promotes and sells young urban gospel music. This isn't your grandmother's gospel music . . . unless your hip grandmother listens to gospel rap!

Charlene built www.gospellinks.com to work with independent gospel artists in a way that wasn't currently available to them in the mainstream gospel world. She provides tons of free information on her web site to help artists develop their own businesses.

Gospellinks.com also makes individual artist pages available for a modest fee, so that artists can directly market themselves to potential fans, and urban gospel fans can buy copies of CDs that ordinarily would be hard to find in the mainstream world.

Another revenue source for Charlene is working with event planners to provide gift bags that include giveaway gospel CDs. That helps the artists get their work out there to a larger audience and Charlene sells advertising on the CD cases themselves!

But wait, doesn't Charlene have to compete with the biggest guy on the online block—Amazon.com? Yes and no. Fans could go to Amazon.com if they already know the names of the artists or CDs they wanted to buy. But wouldn't a dedicated fan prefer to go browse Charlene's site and learn more about the artists themselves? And wouldn't the fans start to share information among themselves and market Charlene's web site for her? Yes. Remember, Amazon.com is only a standard retailer, a music store online. Charlene is building her own world in which fans, artists, and managers can all meet and benefit.

So ask yourself, what niche is missing in the online music world? Are you a fan of an obscure or non-mainstream type of music? Perhaps there is a weekend business for you! Check out Charlene's web site and learn from her impressive technique.

High-End Sheet Sales

How does this sound for a wonderful life—Robin Powers lives and works out of a 1964 converted bus known as "Big Blue Betty" which lets her live and work full time all over the country. She sells a luxury product—1,000 thread count, organically grown

Egyptian cotton bed sheets—on eBay. And she does it the lazy way, working only two to three hours a day, which allows her to pull in a comfy six figure salary.

Using satellite internet and cell phones to stay in touch with friends, family, and business associates, Robin enjoys life on her own terms while she travels the country. In the past, she struggled and didn't have the luxuries and peace of mind that her eBay business affords her today. Robin was coming off of a divorce and had to figure out how to support herself after a decade of hobbies and failed businesses during her marriage. It took some wandering around before she stumbled across eBay.

A friend told her that she could buy ski passes in October for $59 and sell them in January for $120, so she bought ten and sold them. This was so easy Robin looked around for what else she could sell. It didn't take her long to explore the merits of drop shipping as an easy way to do business on eBay. After discovering that eBay is an expansive marketplace where customers come looking for you and what you have to offer, she was ready to begin a life that was not only simple and easy but financially rewarding.

All and all, it cost Robin a couple of thousand dollars to get her business going, and like many newbies, she had an unexpected setback a year and a half after she started her business. She charged the $5,000 she needed to fix the problem on a credit card. Thanks to her successful business, she was able to recover that money before the credit card bill payment was due. A feat that may have been almost impossible to pull off with the typical "day job."

Robin takes great pride in offering superior customer service and exquisite quality. The cotton for the long-staple Egyptian Cotton sheets and bedding that she sells is hand picked, not machine picked. Check them out at www.Elegantbeds.com. This, Robin points out, prevents the individual fibers from becoming broken and frayed by the machinery, resulting in longer, softer fabric. Every step in the manufacture of these fine linens uses 100 percent organic materials. The cotton is grown completely pesticide-free, the dying is performed with all natural materials, and even the bleaching is done with no chemicals, using a compound made from seashells. Excellence and her reasonable pricing has helped Robin's business rise to the top.

Selecting the right product shouldn't stop anyone from getting started if they want to sell a product on eBay. She says "Yes, it just takes some perseverance. Finding a great product can really take time. So when I coach others to do what I do, we work to find something quickly, even if it's not the perfect product. I find that getting items sold quickly keeps folks motivated. And it teaches the entire process of the business from sourcing products, to posting, to customer service."

She eventually took classes, but that was after her business was successful. Like the owners of many revenue generating businesses on the cutting edge of change, Robin stays on top by continuing to add new sources of income in the form of web sites, affiliate sales, and her e-book "Sell on eBay THE LAZY WAY! Make a Living in Just Two Hours a Day," and on her web site www.auction-diva.com.

Imported Watches

Marc Frankel has always been a watch enthusiast, so selling imported watches was a natural extension of something that he enjoys. Marc and his wife were pleasantly surprised when he turned a profit with his first sale because his operating expenses were (and continue to be) extremely low. The first order of watches from Europe cost him about $800.

In mid-2003, Mark, an Aerospace Engineer, with help from his wife, an accountant, launched a low-maintenance yet highly profitable part-time business that raked in $85,000 last year.

Marc started by selling imported watches on eBay. By December of that year, he opened his web site www.longisland watches.com, and knock on wood, he is still in business today.

While Marc and his wife both continue to work full time, revenues from Island Watch are soaring. Marc takes care of the web work and order fulfillment when he gets home at night and on the weekends. It takes roughly 20 hours a week for this couple to generate an extra full-time income.

Island Watch imports wristwatches from around the world and sells them at low prices. They are popular sellers because the quality and features in the wristwatches are generally found in watches costing many times their prices. And their customer service is simply the best, with a no-questions-asked return policy.

Marc credits his intuition as his best resource. The idea for Island Watch stemmed from reading the book *Rich Dad, Poor Dad*. His business is basically a one-person operation. He conceived the idea out of the blue, designed a web site, and does everything the business currently needs. While Marc says his business model is rudimentary at best, it is simple and can be duplicated by anyone who has a niche item to sell.

Internet and Affiliate Marketing Consultant

In 1997, if anyone had told Rosalind Gardner that clicking on a banner ad with the words "Webmasters Make Money" would change her life, she would have called him crazy. Not only was she completely ignorant about doing business on the internet, she had no business experience in the real world either.

As an air traffic controller, all Rosalind had to do was work another 20 years and retire with a comfortable pension. But as fate would have it, all of that changed. In May of 2000, that little banner ad prompted Rosalind to leave her job—including giving up the comfort and security of having a pension. She clicked on that banner ad and it took her to the signup page that explained that webmasters could earn commissions by selling dating service memberships. Having spent a few bleak evenings in internet chat rooms, Rosalind saw value in a service that lets singles meet

Affiliate Program: Another Way to Earn Passive Income

You can create a different form of passive income on the internet by selling information products such as ebooks. Another way to make money is to sell someone else's product or service using what is called an affiliate program. The company with the product(s) gives you a special link for your web site so they can track sales and pay you a commission for each sale, and this creates a stream of passive income for you. When you are getting started this may require time, effort, and a small amount of money, but once it is set up your business is on autopilot.

The reverse works too. You can set up an affiliate program of your products and services and other web sites can make money by having you on their web sites creating a win-win.

other singles based on location, education, age, and a wide array of other variables.

Joining the affiliate program was free, so Rosalind decided to give building a web site that reviewed internet dating services a try. She had to learn everything from scratch, from building pages, reviewing dating services, and finding ways to get visitors to her site. She was determined to make this business a success.

Her determination paid off quickly. Six weeks after the site was launched, an envelope from her affiliate arrived in the mail. Inside was a check for $10.99. That check proved to Rosalind that she could make money online, and she was inspired to work even harder.

From her humble beginnings, in June 2003 Rosalind went on to publish her first book, *The Super Affiliate Handbook: How I Made $436,797 Last Year Selling Other People's Stuff Online*. Check it out at www.netprofitstoday.com.

Rosalind is a big fan of selling-online-as-an-affiliate program. There are no product development costs, and building a web site is dirt-cheap compared to what a bricks-and-mortar store would cost to build. You don't have inventory to carry, there are no orders to process, and no products to ship—the merchant does all of that. They also take care of customer service. It's free to sign up as an affiliate, and there are thousands of merchants who want you to promote their products. Everyone from 1-800-Florals and Disney, to Verizon and Ziff Davis have affiliate programs.

You are only limited by your imagination because the potential for niche affiliate sites are endless. According to Rosalind, the best part about affiliate marketing, is that you really can make money while you sleep. Day or night, people from around the world can come to your site and buy, and you'll never have to stand at a till.

Garage Sales for Online Profits

Everyone has a friend or neighbor who has done it—found an inexpensive item for sale at a garage sale or flea market, dusted it off, posted it on eBay, and lo and behold, it sold for a ton of dough! Great, now get up every Saturday morning and try to do it again and again . . .

You've read several descriptions of folks who run concentrated businesses on eBay, selling high-end sheets, imported watches, or custom vintage gift baskets. What about the hardworking folks who take potluck at what they can find and resell? Is it still possible to make extra money buying and selling miscellaneous items on eBay? You bet!

Have you run across Lynn Dralle on your television set, or maybe in the pages of *The National Enquirer*, or perhaps on her blog at www.thequeenofauctions.com? Lynn is an eBay Power-Seller who sometimes sells up to $20,000 a month, all items she has found in her own community and sold online at a profit.

Opportunities abound for items that can be bought inexpensively and sold for a profit. Although it seems sometimes like the whole world is online and selling stuff on eBay, there is still an endless market. Because it all depends on what a prospective buyer is out there looking for . . . one day it might be used skateboard clothing for a young boy (something Jennifer buys frequently!) and the next day it might be missing pieces of your grandmother's china pattern. Even if millions of people have millions of items listed for sale, millions more are hopping online to buy!

Check out *Start Your Own Business on eBay* by Jacquelyn Lynn (Entrepreneur Press, 2004) for a solid introduction to how to get up and running quickly with an auction business. The truly great thing about conducting auctions on eBay is that you are always in control over how much time and effort you put into it. Don't feel like going out one weekend to look for potential items? Fine, skip it and try to find twice as much stuff the next week. One thing you can't be casual about though, is handling other people's money and orders. Once you have sold something online to a customer and taken his or her money, you cannot be casual about exactly when you get down to the post office to ship it out. You need to be 100 percent professional about the selling aspect of your eBay business or you will quickly find yourself on the wrong end of not only the eBay feedback system, but also laws regarding mail-order businesses.

Wedding Favors

In January 2004, Jennifer Fallon and her husband Brad launched their first online store using a $50-per-month Yahoo! Store. After they built the store and entered their initial products, they sold over $10,000 during their first month. By April they had over $80,000 in monthly sales and had to find a warehouse to hold their inventory. In May, sales had reached $132,000, and by June they were bringing in over $150,000 per month and had to upgrade their warehouse. Now they have a full-time staff of six and Jennifer still works at home. Their gross sales have already reached $1 million for www.myweddingfavors.com.

One thing they discovered was that despite the setbacks of the 1990s, you can still open an eCommerce business and have it become a huge success. But Jennifer says there are some factors to consider when you are getting started.

Step 1: Find a High Demand Niche Market

When Brad and Jennifer were married in May of 2003, Jennifer wanted to be able to have children and stay at home without giving up her income. But she had a corporate software sales job that included a lot of travel. The initial idea for the new business came to her when she was planning her own wedding and was looking for placecard holders for their reception. As she surfed the web, she thought "What a great internet business—wedding favors. People are looking to purchase large quantities for the entire guest list, and you can't exactly walk into a store and buy 150 personalized candles. Plus, there are so many items on your wedding planning checklist that it's ideal to be able to go to the internet on a Sunday night in your pajamas and knock an item off the list."

She decided to do more research on this online market, and using the free "Search Term Suggestion Tool" at www.over ture.com, Jennifer found that over 100,000 people per month were searching for the term "wedding favors." Jennifer says "I knew it had potential. In addition, my husband had experience in something called Search Engine Optimization—helping web site owners get their web sites to the top of the search engines. So it seemed that an online business selling wedding products was going to be a great fit."

Step 2: When You Have What People Want, Make Sure They Know About It

How are you going to find 100,000 people a month who may be searching for what you are selling? That is where Jennifer and

Brad began to strategize with the new business. Brad had been experimenting with different techniques to get a web site a higher ranking in the search engines. He put into practice some theories he had developed as one of the leading experts in the search engine field. They started moving up in the search results almost immediately.

First they noticed they were coming up on page 3 on Google, so they kept working at it and the next thing they knew, mywed dingfavors.com, was coming up in the #1 slot on Yahoo! and #2 on Google when somebody searched for "wedding favors."

Very shortly thereafter profits started to soar. They went from six to ten orders a day to 50 to 60 orders a day, selling over $160,000 per month! Their little side business was now a million dollar enterprise. Jennifer went from having a few products in their basement and help with shipping from her retired father to a large warehouse with six employees.

Jennifer attributes the success of her company to search engine marketing, "Think about it—people perform a web search for a product when they are ready to buy it. It's the best form of targeted marketing there is. In our case the word "wedding" is the fifth most commonly searched phrase on the internet. It is searched for more than 3,000 times a month on Google alone. And out of more than 822,000 listed web sites that sell wedding favors, our site comes up well ahead of our competition. The power of advertising using search engine marketing has proven to be so powerful to us that it is now our primary form of marketing and advertising. And Brad has gone on to start his own company devoted to creating high search engine rankings for web sites, SEO Research."

Step 3: Know When to Outsource

Jennifer originally started this business as a sideline endeavor. It quickly started to take over her life. One of the first lessons she had to learn was that if her business was to remain a success, she couldn't do it all by herself. Orders were piling up, but there was no way she could handle order processing, shipping, bookkeeping, and still maintain a high level of customer service.

Jennifer had to delegate some of the day-to-day duties to continue to grow. "Now that I have a staff to handle the more labor-intensive details, this is quickly becoming the work-at-home opportunity I dreamed of. I have the freedom to do the things I want in life, and the satisfaction of owning my own business. While I would never say that running this type of company is easy (because it isn't), I do know that it can be intensely rewarding and personally satisfying. If you're looking for a homebased business with a high-yield potential, then I highly recommend eCommerce as the way to build your path to success."

■　■　■　■　■

What Can You Start?

Jennifer Fallon of WeddingFavors.com just walked us all through some of her steps to success. So much of what she went through is typical of all of the online entrepreneurs we talked to, and is valuable advice for making any online business a success.

Do any of the online businesses we've outlined sound inspiring to you? Although we do believe that actual physical businesses can be duplicated in a good-sized community—that you can open a used bookstore in a town that might already have one, for instance—the online world is one big, big community. We don't recommend trying to replicate these exact ideas and compete head-to-head online with the businesses we've interviewed and featured.

Instead, look for the qualities that made each one succeed. Was it the personal passion for the product (unicycles!), was it years of accumulated compliments that finally gave someone the confidence (coffee cakes!), or perhaps it was the chance to take knowledge and skills and make them available to a larger potential client base (online coaching!)?

Remember that having a beautiful web site isn't enough. You don't make money online unless someone not only comes to your web site but you make a sale. Our friends at www.marketing tips.com have a web site stuffed with good information about successfully marketing a web-based business. They strongly recommend using the powerful marketing research available for free on the Google search engine.

Try looking at these free tools found on the Google toolbar:

- *Google Groups search.* This is great for product or market research, as you can search for your keywords within the thousands of Google Groups online and find forums relevant to your web site. By checking these forums regularly, you'll get to know what's important to the people in your target market.
- *Search News.* This feature lets you find news stories relevant to your web site, e-zine, or blog within news pages indexed by Google. It's great for sparking content ideas or just keeping up with the latest developments in your market or industry.
- *Web Directory search.* This option lets you search Google's directory for sites that match your search terms. It's ideal for finding out how many competitors you may have for a new product, and for seeking out potential linking partners.
- *Search Froogle.* Froogle lets online shoppers search for products and compare prices. It displays pictures, prices, and links to online stores in the results, so you can use it to quickly research how the pricing of your products or services compares with other offerings across the web. If

you have an idea for a new product, Froogle is a great place to check out your potential competitors.

Once you get the hang of them, these powerful tools can become a great asset to your business, as they can save you hours spent on research—leaving you more time to concentrate on developing new products, new marketing strategies, and other ways to boost your profits.

Our final chapter of business ideas focuses on how to market your knowledge and skills—by teaching classes, organizing seminars, and selling info products. Read on and learn how you could become a weekend *infopreneur*!

6

SIGN 'EM UP

Designing Seminars, Boot Camps, Events, Classes, and Other Ways to Market Knowledge and Expertise

After three chapters stuffed with examples of intriguing weekend businesses, we are in the final stretch. The following 25 businesses are based on knowledge, on profiting from your own expertise and level of knowledge in ways that were never before possible. Over the years, the ways to profit off of your own knowledge have grown and expanded. Whereas many years ago you would have marketed your expertise in a high-end newsletter like Andrew Harper's Hideaways travel letter, or perhaps recorded an inspirational or informational hour long talk, now you can dash off a 20-page ebook or lecture 100 people by phone at once! Technology and inventiveness have really come into play in this category.

Jennifer and Michelle both spend a considerable amount of time professionally with Mark Victor Hansen (the co-author of the amazing *Chicken Soup for the Soul* books) and are in wonder at the way he conducts large-scale teleseminars, weekend boot-camps, and mentoring programs. Extraordinary sums of money change hands in the back of the room as all manner of materials are sold and classes are enrolled in. "How'd he think of that?" we both ask ourselves constantly as we witness yet another amazing display of business acumen. And then we get busy trying to duplicate it ourselves!

Ask yourself this critical question: What do you know that others would be willing to pay you to teach them? There needs to be an interest in your skill, topic, or expertise before you can try to market yourself or materials based on your knowledge.

The Queen of Auctions

Remember the criteria for success in this chapter? That you possess a skill or knowledge that others seek? That you are an absolute expert in a sexy topic? Well, what about those millions of us seeking success in online auctions? Isn't that an amazing market right there?

You bet it is for Lynn Dralle, the self-proclaimed Queen of Auctions. Although her web site contains lots of free information on auction success, she will also happily sell you a DVD for $24.95 so that you too can experience the same kind of success.

You can find out what the knowledge products are that Lynn markets by visiting her web site at www.thequeenofauctions.com.

Not only does Lynn make instructional DVDs available, she has also developed tracking sheets to help you run your eBay auctions more smoothly and stay on top of all of the action.

To develop and sell an instructional DVD, do you have to sink thousands into equipment and production? Do these have to be super high quality productions?

Well, you don't want it to be totally amateurish, resembling a high-school film student's first effort. But neither does it have to be Hollywood quality. Remember, you are selling information, valuable information, and as long as your video delivers what it promises—good, solid, how-to information—your customer will be happy.

Jess Todtfeld—The Pitch Doctor

Jess has a job that is envied all over America—he is a segment producer for the super hot network *Fox News* in New York. In addition to his fulltime gig at Fox, he is also known in the media world as "The Pitch Doctor." What does a pitch doctor do? A pitch doctor works with folks who want to beef up their appeal to the media. Even if you have a great story for the media, you need to know how to "pitch" yourself in such a way that producers will want to book you on their shows.

Jess runs his side business from his web site, www.successin media.com. He sells his time as a consultant in three-hour chunks, coaching folks who can't come and spend a full eight hours with him at a day-long seminar over the phone and through e-mail. Future plans include a long-term mentoring program for a monthly fee.

What works in a big way for both Jess and his clients is the day-long seminar. A recent seminar was organized by a publicist who had complementary skills and expertise. She marketed the seminar and together they had ten participants for an eight-hour Saturday session. Just ten folks? Not a problem, as each of those people had paid $1,000 to be there and learn. That's right, $10,000 for one full day's work.

Putting together day-long seminars can be very profitable. "Don't let your group get too big," Jess warns, "Ten is a nice size. Everybody gets enough personal attention. Twenty-five is too big. These people are paying for personal attention; they are buying time with you. They won't be happy having to share you with a huge group."

Working fulltime with Fox News Channel and actively fathering two young children doesn't leave too many free hours for Jess, but he has found a way to do it all. Jess squeezes in most of his extra income time in odd hours—"I commute in to New York City on the train, so I can work on e-books and material for CDs." He plans to add more products to his mix, so that he can create income from product instead of always having to sell his time as a consultant.

Teach Handyman Skills

In Chapter 3, we covered the idea of selling your handy talents and skills on a weekend business, renting yourself out on an hourly basis as a "rent a husband." Well, if you are that handy, perhaps in addition to charging folks to fix their problems, you can also charge folks to teach them a few skills.

Organizing classes on how to do common household repairs are always popular, and there is a large surge now in the numbers of women who want to learn how to fix things around the home. Tailoring your class for seniors, women, or teens could help you narrow your focus and market more effectively.

In the space of an afternoon you could bring your students up to speed on how to:

- Handle a power drill
- Fix a leaky faucet

- Stop a running toilet
- Unclog a toilet
- Replacing switches and plugs
- Basic sprinkler system upkeep

Target eight or ten basic household skills and build your lessons around them instead of trying to cram too much information into the space of just a few short hours.

An offshoot of this is to put together a weekend seminar on how to clean your house faster, better, and cheaper. Remember, people like to save time and money on unpleasant tasks! Teach homeowners how to clean their houses from top to bottom in 45 minutes and you will have customers lined up! With either handyman or cleaning skills, you might find that your students decide to hire you to handle these things for them after all!

Market your classes by putting up small signs in local hardware stores and grocery stores (always check first with the manager) and writing a catchy press release for your local newspaper.

Concierge Consultants

Remember the concierge business idea from Chapter 3? Setting up a part-time business helping folks with miscellaneous errands and personal services sounds like a fun way to make extra money, but did it sound too overwhelming to get started? Not to worry, there are a few hardworking consultants who will teach you how to do it yourself, for a consulting fee between $5,000 to $8,000. How's that for profiting off of your knowledge?

Katharine Giovanni and her husband Ron started a concierge business in 1998 and spent a long hard year figuring it all out without benefit of books, manuals, or consultants. Once they got their business on the success track others began to ask Katharine for advice. Her husband pointed out that she shouldn't be giving away all that advice for free, so Katharine set out to profit from her hard-won knowledge. She wrote books, manuals, and organized seminars. And she became a consultant.

A full-day seminar with Katharine on how to start a concierge business runs $445. Not too bad, eh?

Are you in a business that appeals to a lot of other people? Do you spend a lot of time fielding questions about how to do what you do? Maybe you shouldn't be giving away all that advice for free! Follow Katharine's example and set up a consulting business to run seminars, sell manuals, and hourly coaching.

You might develop a successful weekend business based on one of the ideas in this book and then be able to build a seminar business around teaching other people how to earn an extra income in the very same way you have!

Selling Secrets

Selling secrets . . . doesn't that sound provocative? We don't know about the provocative part, but it can certainly be lucrative!

We've been discussing the various ways to sell your knowledge and expertise in order to generate an extra income. But what if you don't possess the types of knowledge that other people will pay for? Well, you could go out and interview someone who does have the kind of knowledge that people will pay for, and create a business around that! How does that work, you ask? Like this:

1. Determine a topic that will sell in DVD, CD, or ebook format through online promotion.
2. Discover an expert in that field who does not already have a product to sell.
3. Approach the expert and propose that you will help him or her develop and market a product for a substantial part of the profits.

This is a technique advocated by Janet Switzer (www.instant income.com), a top mentor to consultants, coaches, and entrepreneurs. She believes that knowledge products can be created easily by following these three steps. Can you see how this would work? Even if you aren't an expert in the field of real estate sales, you could interview the top sellers and create an ebook or CD called "Sales Secrets of Mega Real Estate Agents." Even if you don't know the first thing about insurance sales, you could create "Million Dollar Insurance Sales Secrets" the exact same way. Think of the endless variations on this theme!

Mahesh Grossman isn't a television producer, he runs a ghost writing business, www.AuthorsTeam.com. He noticed how interested his writing clients were in the idea of appearing on public television. It seems we all want to be the next PBS pledge program superstar like Suze Orman or Wayne Dyer. Instead of shrugging his shoulders and staying in his own narrow field, Mahesh decided instead to go out and create a product to fill this need. He interviewed top public television producers about what it takes to make a show work on public television, and what steps you would need to take to get there. Mahesh is currently producing the CD version of the interviews he conducted and plans to offer "How to Become a Public Television Star" to the 20,000 members of his online newsletter for a hefty $250.

Look around, who do you admire? Who has phenomenal success that you think others will want to emulate? What secrets do you really want to know that you think others will also? Track those secrets down and profit from them!

Information Technology Seminar Training Company

"Give great service. Find out what people want and give it to them in a way that creates the WOW factor." That's the principle used by Paul Browning, owner of Networks Incorporated, Ltd. of England, to build his business and provide customers the level of service that keeps them coming back for more. Paul started his information technology training and consulting business in July 2002 in his spare time. His web site is at www.networksinc.co.uk.

Paul, already employed in the IT support business, realized he could teach the stuff he knew to other companies or individuals. He started his teaching business on weekends. That gave Paul the opportunity to grow his business while maintaining a steady, albeit small income from his employer. In just a few short months, Paul was able to earn more money in two days then he could in two months working for what soon became his former employer. Fearful that his boss would feel threatened and fire him before he was ready, Paul told no one of his new venture until he was ready to quit. That's sage advice for any entrepreneur, especially one planning to work in the same industry as his or her employer.

Networks Incorporated turned an immediate profit. A couple of things worked in Paul's favor. His initial investment in the business was labor as opposed to cash. He wrote the course himself and managed to acquire most of the equipment to teach his classes for next to nothing. Second, Paul was able to run the business from his home. Only on training days did he need to rent a room to teach. Due to his low overhead, Networks Incorporated could be run for a fraction of the cost of most competitors and still turn a profit.

Today Paul earns a comfortable six-figure income. In the early stages he reinvested a sizable portion of his profits into marketing courses and more equipment so that his students had a better experience in the training course.

Paul's advice: Avoid the mentality that spending money in your business and educating yourself to be an entrepreneur is bad. He also cautions not to waste money on flashy cars, top-of-the-line laptops, and other things that only serve to make you feel more successful rather than provide any real benefit to the business. And finally, always ask for referrals and give a referral fee.

Sewing Instructor

Pamela Tripaldi is the founder of "You Can Make It." Hundreds of parents have begun to earn money from home by teaching sewing, using lesson plans and instructional videos from "You Can Make It," found at www.youcanmakeit.com. When reflecting on her priorities in life, Pamela says, "My children are gifts that God has given me. My first obligation is to nurture those gifts. The second gift that I got was sewing. I am very lucky to be able to work with all the gifts that I was given, and to help other people achieve that dream also."

After many years of being home with her daughters, Pamela felt the need for a creative outlet. "I wanted to do something, but didn't want to work full time. Having been involved with sewing since my teen years, I decided in 1992 to approach my local fabric store and ask if I could offer sewing lessons." The classes were very successful and after offering sewing lessons locally she realized that teaching others to sew is something that other people could do. Pamela says, "After two years of writing into the wee hours of the morning, my seven-level sewing curriculum was complete. I started marketing it nationally in 1994. This was the beginning of my company, 'You Can Make It.'" Her girls have been in each video and with the help of a teacher, or just by watching the videos, anyone can learn to sew.

Pamela no longer has time to offer sewing lessons personally, but her business keeps her very busy. She has over 300 teachers using her curriculum. Most of them are in the United States, but they also have affiliates in China, Canada, and other countries. Pamela's office is in her home, and she employs local high-school students to help her after school so she can spend time with her kids, now 13 and 12.

"You Can Make It" is structured so that people can earn extra income by using this program to help them offer sewing lessons. The program supplies everything that an experienced seamstress needs to teach. There is a one-time purchase price for the program, with no franchise, monthly, or student fees. The teacher's initial cost is minimal and is usually recouped in one to three months. Pamela suggests, "Teachers need two or three sewing machines, which we recommend they borrow from friends until their income is sufficient to purchase their own. Teachers pay a small yearly fee to continue to receive student referrals, our newsletter with pattern suggestions, and all updates to our program." People can offer lessons at a local fabric stores, community centers, churches, or in their own homes. Some of their teachers offer free classes at shelters for abused women, in jails, or in other community service settings. The curriculum includes commercially available patterns, so there is no need to keep returning to "You Can Make It" to buy supplies. A teacher usually has four in a class but can go up to six (more than six students is not recommended).

The average teacher charges $42.50 a month and is earning $850 per month for five hours of work per week, with four students per one hour class.

Sewing is becoming popular again, adults and children enjoy learning to sew. In addition to being a wonderful hobby, sewing can be a means for anyone to become financially independent. With the skill of sewing, prospects are wide open in home decorating, alterations, dressmaking, and designing. All are excellent avenues for providing extra income, especially if you want to structure a life around family.

Online Piano Lessons

Learn the proven secrets to instantly playing any song by ear on the piano—gospel, jazz, R&B, country, soul, and more! If you want to learn what it takes to propel your piano playing to the next level, then you can't afford to miss these online piano lessons.

Wow! How can you resist that appeal? Thousands of folks haven't been able to resist the appeal of the online piano lessons available from 22-year-old business wunderkind Jermaine Griggs. A youth pastor who just recently finished college, Jermaine has been playing the piano and leading choirs since he was nine. In order to spread his own joy in music, he began to develop new techniques to teach others what came so effortlessly to him.

Jermaine's web site is very sophisticated when it comes to making the sale. He offers "free lessons" that will grab the attention of online visitors and hopefully bring them back to buy the whole package once they've given it a try. In addition, when a visitor logs onto his site, a box appears that offers a super deal if the visitor signs up in the first five minutes of his or her visit to the www.hearandplay.com site. A small clock let's you know just how much time remains until the special deal expires, a very effective technique. Check out his site thoroughly to see what kinds of tips you can glean about selling courses online.

Seminar Business

After spending just a few minutes talking to Stephen Pierce, you get the impression that he'll never have to worry about making a good living again because everything he touches turns to gold. Stephen candidly reflects on his past . . . *"BLAM! The shot rang out, I fell to the ground . . . laying there bleeding, I knew it was time for a change."* Five years later, he is running a multimillion-dollar homebased business.

Like many people who want to have their own prosperous home business, Stephen tested a variety of business opportunities. He drifted from failure to failure, always trying to find the easy way out. He was unsuccessful at each business he started including vinyl repair, arbitration, mail order, a homebased telemarketing business selling coupon books that helped consumers reduce their grocery bills, and many more. Once homeless, this high school dropout didn't let his tenth grade education drive a wedge between him and the American Dream.

Stephen Pierce started out teaching people how to attain success on the internet with his Rapid Fire Swing Trading strategy. This wasn't a direction he was planning to take, but an online peer saw the financial success he was enjoying and offered to pay him $5,000 to learn his methodology. His web site and a coaching club was soon to follow, and Stephen finally found the success he had long searched for. Next, he wrote a 49-page ebook, charged $49, and made $50,000 on the internet in one month.

As a weekend entrepreneur, Stephen recently started giving seminars that teach entrepreneurs to formulate creative and innovative marketing strategies. His experiences along the bumpy road to success helped him discover a solution to the lack of resources most small businesses are burdened with. They don't have access to creativity and innovation—which Stephen says is the backbone of large companies such as Apple and Starbucks.

When Stephen gave his first Creativity and Innovation seminar he made a huge profit. He credits his success to building relationships with people, and the fact that they trust him and know his products and services work. But go deeper and there is a business philosophy that Stephen talks about that most of us could benefit from. The real competition he says is found within a company's business model. And these are the examples he gives: "Hotmail surpassed America Online with subscribers and Microsoft bought them for their business model. Both creativity and innovation help us recognize where people are going tomorrow." He adds, "Starbucks has a completely different business model and turned the market upside down. It's not about the product or service, it is the experience that Starbucks devotees crave. Dunkin Donuts sell donuts—Starbucks sells an experience."

Stephen has stayed ahead of the competition by observing the needs of small- to medium-sized businesses and filling these needs by providing information that helps them grow exponentially. His web site is www.innovationmarketers.com.

Publisher of Journals

LifeBio's founder and president, Beth Sanders, became intrigued with the power of a person's life story after an impromptu tape-recorded interview with her grandmother in 1994. Through the interviewing process, Beth gained a new perspective and stronger connection with this average but extraordinary woman who had experienced life throughout most of the 20th century. Due to the profound effect this information had on Beth and her family, she built a business around helping people share family traditions and values.

To help create her business Beth took a class in entrepreneurship that motivated her to write a feasibility study on her idea. She got the validation she was looking for and says, "We're definitely benefiting from three trends right now—the proliferation of long-distance families, the aging of America, and the growth of the internet for seniors. LifeBio was the first online legacy creation company." Today, over 4,000 people use LifeBio's products and services, but Beth's goal is to empower millions to tell their own and others' life stories.

People like the process LifeBio uses to gather information. Beth says, "Most people are so overwhelmed by the thought of recording their personal history that they don't know where to begin, and they simply never get started. We encourage people to answer just one question a day." The web site and book are divided into short sections so you can go at your own pace and it is easier and less time-consuming than sitting down to write your memoir or autobiography without any sort of direction.

To accommodate the needs of a wider audience, Beth has a copyrighted workbook version of her web site www.Life Bio.com, with the same questions and format to help simplify transferring the data from the book to the web so that a physical book can be printed. This unique concept was trademarked and copyrighted and Beth has plans to expand this format to include entrepreneurs who want to preserve their own personal business history using LifeBio. Another effective tool that has helped grow her business is a mastermind group. It helps her create innovative strategies and new ways to increase sales and public awareness that she would not have been able to achieve alone.

LifeBio recently had a growth spurt from an Associated Press story that ran in hundreds of papers last spring. The article brought lots of traffic to her web site, some became immediate buyers while others subscribed to her free newsletter and will, she hopes, eventually buy from LifeBio. Beth feels this is an ideal business because she can easily juggle parenting with working approximately 25 hours a week. She says "The gross margin on a web-based service like this is significantly higher than any other business I know of."

Etiquette Classes

Jennifer's son was recently the youngest guest at a formal dinner. During the first course he quietly raised his hand, indicating that he wished to speak. Jennifer was beside herself with pride at this obvious display of good manners. "Yes?" the dignified host asked him. "I don't like this soup," the honest six-year-old said loudly. So much for parental pride!

How are your manners? Do you have a deep enough understanding of proper behavior and etiquette in all manner of situations to be able to teach others who are seeking to polish their own social skills? If so, you might have an educational business close at hand.

What do etiquette instructors do? They help inform the uninformed on topics like:

- Proper introductions
- Handshake methods
- Table etiquette
- Social and communication skills
- Proper host and guest behavior

Nowadays it is considered critical in the business world to have a firm grasp of proper etiquette, and many a newly hired executive has gone looking for a course to fill in the social blanks. Sometimes the suggestion even comes from the personnel department!

To teach etiquette courses, you do need to have a thorough grasp of the concepts yourself, of course. If you'd like a refresher course yourself that will also teach you how to run a business like this, here are two different schools that will train you for a fee and give you the necessary tools to become an etiquette instructor to both children and grownups.

The Protocol School of Washington
(877) 766-3757
www.psow.com

The American School of Protocol
(404) 252-2245
www.theamericanschoolofprotocol.com

Dispute Resolution

Joy Bounds made the decision to start a conflict resolution and dispute prevention business after she repeatedly observed the need to resolve conflicts in a mutually agreeable manner without the expense and consternation often caused by the legal system. With an investment of $2,000 for office equipment, Joy's business has been running like a fine-tuned race car for ten years. From the beginning, her mediation company has been profitable and personally fulfilling. Joy spends part of her time negotiating contracts at her job which has now become a part-time position giving her the time and flexibility to spend 20 hours a week on her side business. Her business has built its reputation on integrity and an ethical approach. With this philosophy, Joy's business has grown using word-of-mouth and paid referrals; she doesn't advertise nor does she have a web site.

Providing mediation services has many benefits for Joy's clients. Her services are considerably less expensive, more efficient, and quicker than retaining lawyers and legal firms with mediation components. Another selling point is that she provides complete confidentiality. Joy says "With me as a dispute neutral, it is an advantage to business people in sensitive dispute situations that otherwise might run the risk of becoming a high profile, media magnet." Joy's experience and caring attitude has given her an edge over many of her competitors. She always puts her clients' needs first, she offers flexible meeting times, and a variety of locations including teleconferencing, video conferencing, and remote communicating.

Cookbook Publishing

If happiness is having what you want and wanting what you have, Willie Crawford is the poster guy for creating a winning recipe for success. When the end of his military career in the Air

Force was near, Willie wanted to pursue his dream of owning his own business. He wasn't sure where he would eventually settle down, so it seemed wise to start an internet business. After spending hundreds of hours surfing the world wide web, subscribing to hundreds of e-zines, and purchasing books and courses, Willie launched several web sites. In 1997 he created a web site to sell his soul food cookbook. Today it takes less than five hours a week to run his business and rakes in a six-figure income. Check him out at www.chitterlings.com, where he has created an entire community devoted to eating and cooking soul food!

Willie's goal was to share the soul food recipes he learned while growing up on a farm in North Carolina. Recipes such as collard greens, sweet potato pie, southern pound cake, banana pudding, pinto beans with ham hocks, and tons of others can be found by people who visit his web site. When he first built his site he started out by posting about 20 of these great recipes. Then he invited all web site visitors to join his mailing list and share their favorite recipes with each other. Since then, literally thousand of soul food and old-family recipes have been shared by web site visitors. Proof that when you do what you love—or what you love to eat—success will follow.

His motto is, "do the work once to get paid over and over again" and that is how Willie has turned his love for food into a gold mine. The book sells for $16.95, and Willie's selection of the right affiliate programs and search engines brings tens of thousands of visitors to his web site, especially during holidays and Black History Month. Willie points out that there are no real secrets to success with a knowledge-based business. He says it takes hard work, persistence, and a worthwhile product or service. During his time online, he noticed that his business grew faster when he didn't really concentrate on trying to help others who were trying to start businesses. When he shared his experience and advice freely, he received a lot of unexpected orders.

According to Willie, perhaps the biggest key to his success is discovering that you have to give before you can receive. And the things that he had been taught on his grandmother's knee turned out to be the things he needed to know for creating a successful business on the internet.

Is there a specialty cookbook in you? Years ago a man published cookbook devoted entirely to variations on pecan pie;

Alternative Streams of Income

- *Affiliate programs.* You can sell other people's products or services and receive a commission. You are given a special link for your web site so they can track sales and pay you a commission for each transaction.
- *Information products.* Ebooks and downloadable Special Reports can be sold or given away. Free products can include links to affiliate programs that will pay you a commission. You can also sell CDs and DVDs.
- *Free teleseminars.* Go ahead and record and transcribe them, and you'll have two products to sell.
- *Sell reprint rights.* Charge a one-time fee for your products, ebook, audio, or video, which will give people permission to sell it for the same price to their audience.
- *Google AdSense.* Google ads can generate money if you have a busy web site with hundreds of pages because each time someone clicks on the ad, you are paid a commission.
- *Pay per click campaigns.* You can make extra money with with a campaign for your product or web site. With Google AdWords you create your own ads, choose keywords to help Google match your ads to your audience, and you are paid only when someone clicks on them.
- *Membership web site.* This is the perfect venue if you are an expert in your field and have the ability to attract loyal followers who will pay you a monthly fee to gain access to your expertise, affiliate programs, and products, which can all add more streams of income.

there have been many other single-topic cookbooks that have reached success. The best types of cookbooks have a built-in audience—like fans of southern cooking, or Midwestern potluck suppers, or kosher cuisine—an audience of folks who are devoted to eating that way and seeking out new recipes and information. It would be tough to build this kind of a business around a general cookbook, so choose your topic wisely.

Public Relations and Marketing

When the movie *Titanic* came out on video, Peter Shankman took his rent money and had 500 T-shirts made up that read, "It Sank. Get Over It." He took them to Times Square, one of New York City's most popular spots, and sold 500 T-shirts in six hours. He "leaked" what he did to *USA Today* and they printed the story on the front page of the "Life" section of the paper. The media attention from the newspaper publicity helped Peter sell over 10,000 T-shirts on the web at $15 a shirt. This clever campaign pulled in over $100,000 from Peter's $1,800 investment, which was more than enough to convince him to start The Geek Factory.

A geek is defined as "one who knows everything about everything," and geek fits Peter Shankman to a tee. However, his company isn't your average public relations tech shop. Geek Factory handles consumer products, throws parties for A-List celebrities, produces corporate sponsorships and movie premieres, and if bad press is an issue provides crisis management to revamp a client's tarnished image. Accolades from mainstream media and trade media have put Geek Factory in the spotlight; *PR Week* magazine gave it the nod as runner up for Boutique Agency of the Year.

Geek Factory has had its share of hurdles to overcome; in the late 90s when Tech PR was all the rage, Peter honed his skills and made that his niche. As the industry shifted, Peter expanded to include other services to a variety of industries. The key he says is, "Adoption and adaptation—being able to change what you're doing on a moment's notice, and adopt new strategies and technologies and abilities as they come into vogue. It's what keeps you going, while the dinosaurs fade away." The Geek Factory started in 1998 with one person, one client, and one cat. Since then, they've grown just a little bit—they represent clients all over the world. You can visit their site at www.geekfactory.com.

Therapeutic Hypnosis

Nancy Irwin was trained as an opera singer, but when a local theatre critic praised her comedic talents she decided to take him up on his dare. She moved to New York City and began performing stand-up at dead-end clubs while securing some forgettable acting gigs on the side. Her comedy act eventually caught on, the rooms got bigger, and her dreams grew right along with them. In 1994 she moved to Los Angeles when she heard that Hollywood "needed more blondes." Nancy enjoyed some success in Los Angeles working the clubs and doing several television shows. She even got a gig touring Korea, where she entertained U.S. military troops. It wasn't long before she became the staff emcee at the famous Improv in Los Angeles working alongside such acts as Jerry Seinfeld, Ray Romano, and Damon Wayans.

With too much time on her hands and no signs of a sitcom deal, Nancy started doing volunteer work at Children of the Night, a shelter for sexually abused teenagers in Van Nuys. Nothing could have prepared her for the dramatic change her life took. The work not only led her to begin healing from the sexual abuse she suffered as an adolescent, but it also led to a career epiphany. Nancy went back to school, earned a doctorate in psychology, and now specializes in the prevention and healing of child sexual abuse through therapeutic hypnosis.

When Nancy retired from showbiz, she took a job in Corporate America to pay the bills and to fund her education. While writing her dissertation, she enrolled in hypnosis school and began seeing clients in her "spare time." Within just six months, her client base was burgeoning and she decided it was time to fish or cut bait. She left Corporate America the day she received her "pass" on her dissertation, she got a lease on a small therapy suite, brought in three other therapists to keep her overhead low by sharing the rent, and got on the phone to create business. Nancy spent all of $5,000 to open the doors to her business, and she says it was one of the happiest days of her life.

Teaching Magazine Publishing

Growing a small idea into a multimillion dollar empire might lead some people to believe that Sue Botterill is a sales superstar or a corporate guru. Actually she's just your average mom who loves her family and would rather spend time with them than anything else. This full-time homemaker has become a part-time entrepreneur who left her banking job in the United Kingdom nine years ago when the first of her three children was born.

Feeling the need to contribute to the family income, Sue was in search of ways to earn extra income. She started looking for a job that would be flexible enough to fit around her children without needing to use childcare. And, at the same time she wanted something that she would enjoy. It wasn't long before Sue saw that nothing fit her criteria.

During this period of time, Sue and her husband had relocated from London, to a suburb of Birmingham for his job. New to the area, they didn't know anyone or how to find simple activities for the kids like gymnastics or dance classes, let alone where to get a decent take-out meal. This dilemma was the springboard for the whole idea of starting her own local magazine.

There was a hitch, though. Her husband and their friends were very skeptical about her proposed business venture. Everyone told Sue that if this idea could work, that someone else would already be doing it.

Full of enthusiasm and unwilling to give up what seemed like a good idea, Sue decided to move forward. She made a plan and gave herself a six-week deadline to get the first edition finished. In her spare time, the next few weeks were spent investigating printers, types of paper, format, content, and compiling advertising rates so she could offer cheaper prices than the local papers.

When the first issue of her magazine was complete Sue knew the magazine was extremely profitable earning her £1,800 pounds ($3,400) for a month of work. After the magazines were delivered, the phone didn't stop ringing with local business owners who wanted to advertise and eventually others wanting to start their own neighborhood magazines.

Local demand to duplicate this successful formula led Sue to create a home-study course that she sells to others who want to run their own magazines from their kitchen tables. The first month was by far the hardest for Sue, she worked about 29 hours a week. Now she enjoys working eight to ten hours a week.

Having helped over 300 people set up their own magazines in 2004, Sue Botterill has earned the respect of the business community, her peers, and the media for creating an award-winning business model. Her company, Mymag has increased its popularity with other stay-at-home mothers who want to follow in her footsteps. They are now earning $3,000 to $4,000 a month part-time in the United Kingdom and this year Sue will be branching out to educate people in other parts of the world including the United States.

Sue is yet another talented weekender who has made money teaching others an expert skill, perhaps running one of her magazines is a good fit for you! Visit her web site www.mymag usa.com.

7

STAY FLEXIBLE, STAY FAST

Adapt to Marketplace Changes and Turn on a Dime!

In a previous chapter you learned how newlyweds Jennifer and Brad Fallon launched www.myweddingfavors.com in January 2004 and by 2005, sales were over $4 million. But did they stop there? Nope. The same ingenuity it took to make that business a mega-success helped Jennifer discover yet another incredible niche market that is turning into an even bigger success.

When Jennifer had a staff in place to delegate many of the day-to-day duties to, she was able to focus on finding new niche products. And although search engine marketing is a big key to success, Jennifer says "it is also important that when someone searches for what you are selling on the internet, you actually have the right product at the right price so they don't continue to keep searching after they visit your store." Another key point that helped Jennifer discover her new niche market was that she wanted to provide as much variety to meet all the different bride's tastes. Finding the right product at a reasonable price in quantity was easier said than done.

Niche Marketing

Tracking major trends can lead to you cashing in on untapped niche markets that are lying dormant, waiting to happen. Good niche businesses are easy to start and seldom have to fight the competition—because there usually isn't any. By discovering a niche where you can build your own unique stronghold, you can attract and maintain customers who will pay top dollar for your goods and services.

Once Jennifer realized what her limitations were, she wanted to find a solution. "Wedding favors used to be Jordan Almonds in a cute paper bag, but the market has changed tremendously; there are not many wholesalers that really specialize in wedding and party favors. Now, there are plenty of gift wholesalers but they target retail stores, have a higher price point, and certainly do not target brides who want to spend around $3 for a cute favor."

So, how to produce a cute $3 wedding favor? Jennifer and Brad knew a couple that grew up in Asia and now worked in corporate jobs in Atlanta. Jennifer and Brad broached the idea of designing and importing products from Asia together. The Fallons had the ideas, the other couple had the connections. What started as a few ideas and designs has turned into another company, www.kateaspen.com, which already has a large customer base and is predicted to sell $2.5 million this year.

Jennifer is quick to admit that she has definitely made some sacrifices in terms of time to get Kate Aspen off the ground. But the reward is that she has finally found something she loves to do; she really enjoys the creative part, coming up with cute ideas, hiring local artists to bring ideas to fruition, and bringing them to market.

Jennifer stresses the importance of finding a niche market, and that you have to learn exactly what the customer wants in that market. She says "If there is anything you can do to change or enhance what is available to customers based on your knowledge, then do it."

Their biggest problem at Kate Aspen during their first year certainly was not sales but backorders and operational issues—similar to www.myweddingfavors.com the first year.

Agility and Speed

Why do we think this is important? Because in order to become a successful weekend entrepreneur, you must do two things:

1. Stay flexible
2. Stay fast

What do we mean? That you must be nimble and respond to the marketplace. Remember the cliché "you can't turn a battleship on a dime"? In business, you do *not* want to be a battleship.

By staying flexible, like a small and nimble craft, you will be able to spot changes in your customers' needs and tastes and respond right away. Jennifer Fallon noticed that brides wanted to spend about $3 on cute favors. So why not design and manufacture cute favors for $3?

Stay fast? Yes, if your small and nimble business craft is flexible, you should also be able to stay fast in your responses to changes. Flexibility will help you stay open to the marketplace, rather than stubbornly wedded to your original concept and unwilling to change. And as for fast, you need to be able to translate that flexibility and change in focus quickly, before the opportunity goes away. What if Jennifer had dilly-dallied in her decision to design and manufacturer wedding favors for a low price point? Someone else would have also spotted the opportunity and gotten into the marketplace faster than she did.

Bagging a Win-Win

Ali Spizman wanted to be a handbag designer. A competitive field, and an expensive one to gain entry into. By staying flexible about how that could happen, she built a company that combines talent with heart.

The Handbag of Hope™ got rolling when Ali was 17 years old and traveled to New York with her mom, Robyn, an Atlanta reporter who was appearing on a New York talk show. Ali met Seth Goldberg, CEO of S.B. Cornerstones, a licensing and manufacturing company, which at the time had just completed an accessory line for pop singer Mariah Carey. Ali discussed her ideas for a handbag line with Seth and he was interested. Goldberg and S.B. Cornerstones President, Bennett Kaye assembled a manufacturing team, created samples, and shared them with key buyers.

What makes Ali and her handbags so special is that she took the time to do some research on the internet about nonprofit organizations. Ali didn't just want to become a designer; she also wanted to use this opportunity to support a cause. While exploring different organizations, Ali learned about courageous 12-year-old Hope Stout who had passed away from a rare form of bone cancer. When the Make-A-Wish Foundation® offered Hope her wish, she asked that all the other children in the Charlotte Make-A-Wish chapter be granted their wishes, putting the requests of 155 other wish kids before her own. And when Hope was interviewed on a syndicated

Getting Your Teen Business Started

- Create a cool yet memorable name for your business.
- Make sure your parents approve of the business before getting started.
- Get help from family and friends, especially if you encounter a problem.
- Talk to many people before starting your business to see if they are interested in your product or service.
- Give a discount on your fliers, this is an incentive for people to do business with you.
- Keep a calendar or day planner to keep up with appointments, vendors, and customers.
- Word-of-mouth is a great way to build a business.
- Use posters and fliers to promote your business in your neighborhood, community center, and church.
- Thank-you cards show your customers you care and is a nice reminder for more business.

radio show, the response to her wish to fulfill the dreams of other children resulted in donations from all over the country, amounting to more than $1.1 million in four short weeks.

Inspired by Hope's mission and generous heart, Ali knew what she wanted to do. "I resolved to carry on Hope's voice to raise funds with my new creation the Handbag of Hope, which will benefit the Make-A-Wish Foundation to help grant wishes for children with life-threatening medical conditions." The Make-A-Wish Foundation receives a minimum of 10 percent of the price from each bag sold. Meeting with Hope's mother and sister helped them get involved with the project too. They shared Hope's artwork with Ali and that became the pattern printed on the handbag. Hope's sister Austin designed the hang tag that tells Hope's story.

Some of the other things Ali did to get started included writing a business plan and making sample handbags, "I began by going to the fabric store and making mock-up prototypes of handbags. This was an elementary way to start, but it gave birth to the idea. I also did lots of drawings and kept a notebook detailing all the ideas and my designs. In the beginning, I invested a great deal of time and energy, but my manufacturer did the investing and they get that credit since they had to make up samples which are very expensive." Since Ali is the creator of the idea, she was fortunate to team up with a highly reputable manufacturer who had amazing insight into this project. "I was at the right place at the right time," says Ali, "but Seth believed in me and with his help and the amazing leadership at Claire's who carries the handbags around the world, it came to life. It really took the support of a lot of people. This is a very costly endeavor to pull off and I was very lucky that someone took my idea seriously and cared enough to bring the products to the marketplace." Ali is currently in college at Indiana University; she is majoring in Telecommunications and is continuing to work on her designs and ideas.

The Handbag of Hope is a product line that exemplifies the vision of how teens can impact the world in a beautiful way. The handbags are sold at Claire's and Icing by Claire's and they do an incredible job at each of their stores nationwide. Another positive result of this project is Ali's book *The Power of a Wish* (www.activeparenting.com) that represents Ali's commitment to the Make-A-Wish Foundation, which is celebrating its 25th anniversary. Ali's book features stories of hope, love, and thanks from wish kids, volunteers, and individuals touched by a wish.

Sounds Like Success

Creative folks have an easier time of staying flexible, as it is often a major part of art. You start your painting out one way and it could well end up a different way, and that is OK! Sit down to write a song about your mom and you'll finish up with a song about your brother. So it make sense that a musician would start out with one business and end up with another!

Pat O'Bryan has the best of both worlds. He has a recording contract with ZYX records, a major independent label based in Germany, and he has five CDs in distribution in Europe. Hold on, because that's not the good news—we'll get to that in a minute. He started playing professionally at the age of 16, studied music in college but dropped out to tour with a rock band which opened for Cheap Trick, Heart, and ZZ Top. He later worked in the W.C. Clark Blues Review, which is still the best blues band in Austin. He played with Stevie Ray Vaughan, B.B. King, and Fabulous Thunderbirds, while working with W.C. In 1990 he opened a recording studio and has engineered and/or produced several hundred CDs for various bands and artists. Sounds like a busy guy, doesn't he?

Knowing his backstory will help you appreciate how he brilliantly parlayed his talent and skill from one thing to another. Hopefully you will be invigorated to put your thinking cap on and figure out how you can do the same with your hobby or expertise.

Pat doesn't mind admitting the hard cold facts about the path he has taken: "I've been a professional musician for 30-plus years and although I have a recording contract and tour regularly, I've never 'made it.'" So now he tours for fun thanks to a new stream of income he has created for himself.

His big break came in January 2004 when he started "Milagro Research Institute." Milagro means miracle in Spanish and the company was an overnight success. According to Pat, "compared to the internet marketing business, the music biz sucks, I made more money with a recent public domain promotion than I make in a year from playing music. In three weeks!"

> ### Passive Income
>
> The most common use of the term passive income refers to income generated from real estate rentals, interest, or dividends that does not come from active participation in a business. This is specified by the U.S. tax code.

And that's why as he packs his bags for another band tour in Germany he says "this tour will probably be my last."

Pat's life is filled with contentment because he is using his natural talent and ability to help others. He creates and markets audio products that use binaural beats, custom-designed music, and subliminal affirmations to help people achieve success. He has written several successful ebooks and creates information products, training audios, meditation audios, and he coaches clients all over the globe who want to learn how to duplicate his formula for success. Pat knew he wanted an online business, with passive income that would continue to arrive long after he had put in the time to create the product. His simplistic yet unique point of view has proven to be a winning combination, "I create the products based on what I perceive to be a need in the market. I also choose my projects based on how much fun they are."

Because his joint venture (JV) partners know that he produces quality products, they're happy to promote his products to their lists. This is his primary strategy to get sales. Hooking up with influential marketers can save months and even years of trying to succeed on the internet. At the same time, without Pat's relationships with his JV partners, it wouldn't matter how good his products are, his message would probably fall on deaf ears. He suggests that if you want to further your skills and to learn how to become successful, attending seminars is a good way to meet potential JV partners—and in his case, partners

Joint Venture				
An agreement between two or more businesses to mutually accomplish a business objective. This usually happens for a limited duration of time or for a specific accomplishment, and is intended to terminate upon the completion of the specified project.				

gave Pat the boost he needed, "once you get a run of successful promotions, word gets around. It gets easier to create relationships." This month he earned a little under $30,000. You can learn more about Pat at www.instantchange.com.

Morphing the Mystery

You've read about mystery shopping here in *Weekend Entrepreneur*, you've heard about it on the radio. So what could be new and flexible and fast about being a mystery shopper? Angela Tothill figured out how.

She expanded her work as a mystery shopper by offering two new services to her clients. She is an independent contractor who also does merchandising, and edits mystery shop reports. Angela recognized a great opportunity when she found it, "When I stumbled across mystery shopping and merchandising, I found something I truly enjoyed. I became spoiled about being my own boss and not having to have set office hours. Some weeks I work 30 hours while others I don't work any. More often I work an average of 10 to 15 hours a week."

Like many successful weekend entrepreneurs she evaluated her skills and set out to prove to companies that she had an edge over the competition. Armed with her Gold Certification through the MSPA, Angela had no problem discovering other niche markets she could help. Learning the benefits of merchandising (less narrative, quicker reports, higher pay, guaranteed assignments) made it easy to add an additional stream of income to her business.

For many years she was going to school full time and raising her two boys; therefore, she was not a good candidate for the typical office job because it was imperative that she have flexibility with her schedule. Mystery shopping accommodated the different responsibilities Angela had between family and school. It also allowed her to take time off whenever her family needed extra attention. As a merchandiser, she visits several stores regularly for service calls. Some of her other responsibilities include making sure the product is clean, placed on the store shelf according to specifications, priced correctly, and that the point of purchase (POP) material is updated. Angela says, "It can be for one product or an entire department or it might be for a single visit or regular service calls. I have experience reading planograms, completing product and department resets, cut-ins, face outs, and filling out call reports. In all my experience as a shopper and merchandiser, I have never missed a deadline or cancelled an assignment. My standing is excellent because I believe in professionalism, anonymity, accuracy, objectivity, clarity, and an attention to details. Mystery shopping and merchandising are not hobbies, but professions and should be treated as such."

The first year in the business she did not take jobs regularly but still made a small profit and built her business. Angela says, "the biggest mistake mystery shoppers and merchandisers make is taking every job that comes their way to 'get their feet wet.' Unfortunately, this lowers the fees all around and causes a large burnout rate with new contractors." She quickly learned that she had to stop taking all the lower fee assignments, "I began mystery shopping in September 2001, merchandising in late 2003, and editing in September 2004."

A mystery shopper goes to assigned locations to ensure that the products and/or services, customer service, and cleanliness are up to company standards. This is usually, but not always, an undercover assignment. All guidelines for the assignment must be followed and a professional report must be submitted by the deadline.

Once the report is complete, it is passed on to a mystery shopping editor, who checks reports to make sure proper grammar, punctuation, spelling, and complete sentences are used in the submitted reports and that all "no" answers are explained before the report is submitted to the client. Angela's experience as an associate and copy editor for a newspaper came in handy. She says, "Editing mystery shopping reports is great because there's no traveling, I can do it from home, and the out-of-pocket expense is nil. However, a contractor must prove herself to be competent in reliability and competence in writing past reports before being offered a position as an editor."

Angela has more advice for potential mystery shoppers—never pay for a list of mystery shopping or merchandising companies, the information is available for free online.

To find opportunities, Angela suggests reading the forums and applying to all the companies you find. Even if assignments are not available in a particular area, she says "it's not uncommon for a company to acquire a new client or outbid another company for a particular client. Because of that, it's best to apply to every company so if clients switch companies, the jobs aren't lost. Another great starting place is the Mystery Shop Resources forum: (http://p216.ezboardcom/bmysteryshopresources), which has a wealth of helpful information for shoppers and merchandisers. The members are friendly and willing to help any 'newbie' with a question without belittling or making the person feel stupid. Unfortunately this does happen on some sites." The most important tool needed for merchandising or mystery shopping is a computer since most jobs are applied for and assigned online. Next would be reliable transportation since traveling all over the city is a part of the job. For mystery shopping, a digital or microcassette recorder is a useful device. A clipboard, screwdrivers, and box cutters are a must for many merchandising assignments.

Angela found it easy to launch her business because she already had the computer, transportation, and a digital recorder. Eventually she purchased a digital camera and also bought RoboForm, which is a customized form filler/password keeper. Having hundreds of company user IDs and passwords, Angela says "it would be nearly impossible to remember them all or have them organized and easily accessible without RoboForm."

Call to Freedom

After a rocky start, Dani Johnson was living her dream. A successful business marketer, her organization was large enough and active enough that her income was impressive. Dani was successful because she had found a way to keep the people in her organization fired up. When she sat down to take stock of her life, though, Dani found that she never had enough time to do the part of it she enjoyed most—inspiring others. Was it time to drop everything and become a sales trainer? Flexible and fast in her thinking, Dani decided that it was.

Today she is founder and president of Call to Freedom, a sales training company. Through her coaching and training seminars, Dani has developed several top-producing sales forces and has impacted the lives of tens of thousands of people. She has helped many achieve six and seven figure incomes. Her passion is seeing people break through financial bondage and excuses that stop them from reaching true freedom emotionally, mentally, physically, spiritually, and financially.

Dani's ability to give very specific answers in a direct manner, combined with her raw motivational style, is what sets her apart from other speakers and trainers. The foundation of her teachings and principles are biblically based and you won't hear anything from her that she hasn't personally used or done herself. Dani coaches successful executives, as well as newbie entrepreneurs on a weekly basis.

When she started doing seminars, people who attended saw their incomes double three weeks later. Demand for her training was so popular that her income hit $80,000 a month. What she discovered while training others is that people wanted to bring their parents and friends; they were in search of not only life skills but inner healing. Dani says "seminars are about who you are as a person—throw a mirror up and people get a wake up call—my seminars help people get off the fence and take action." For over 14 years Dani had been asked to train individual companies and she said no. However, she and her husband joined forces and experimented with their www.danijohnson.com web site. This first step catapulted them into the seminar training business a couple of years ago.

When Dani started her business it changed her life forever. After getting the right coaching and training, her income went to $20,000 per month in just five months and now she can teach others how to do the same thing. She also produces and sells videos and audio recordings so people can get the training they need if they can't attend a live seminar. Dani enjoys working 20 hours a week, which gives her time to be a mom and a wife.

Cobbling Up Success

Go to any of the 13 busy farmers' markets in the Los Angeles and you are bound to find a stand selling fresh fruit cobblers. These aren't just any cobblers, mind you, they come from Shae Sewards' company, Cobblermania! Check her out at www.cobbler mania.com.

When Shae was first considering where to sell her cobblers, farmers' markets were appealing in large part because of the flexibility. Remember that word, flexibility? "I wanted to keep overhead low, and I wasn't locked into a long-term contract. Besides, the customers there are motivated to buy and always on the lookout for something different!"

It took about one year before Cobblermania became profitable. "After a year I was able to expand and hire people to run my booths for me and enter more lucrative events. For example, this year Cobblermania will be an exhibitor at the Black Business Expo." During Shae's first year of introducing Cobblermania to the public, she says growing the business was more important than making money "I consider 'profitable' to mean more than just a monetary concern. Cobblermania's profit, for me, also stems from how it continues to transform my life and those who work for me. Every single week, we meet great and interesting people at different events. It's hectic, time-sensitive, challenging, grueling, and oh so worth it. I'm having an absolute blast!"

Shae is now in a period where flexibility is crucial—she is having a hard time meeting demand for her product! "Until recently, we were always selling out everywhere. A few months ago, I was approached by a food marketing field rep about placing Cobblermania cobblers in their outlets. Next, I was asked to start selling them over the internet through a distributor. Time will tell which direction we grow in. As a result, I am now dealing with attorneys who specialize in franchises and national trademarks. Fortunately they are close (childhood) friends or friends of close friends."

By staying open to future possibilities like Shae, looking for opportunities to create the product of your dreams like Ali, or developing new services to offer clients like Angela, your part-time business can remain flexible. Remaining flexible about where your business takes you allows to you stay fast. Make "flexible and fast" your new slogan for the future!

SUCCESS
STRATEGIES

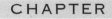

8

REACH
FOR SUCCESS
Learning Strategies that Work

Well, what do you think of all these weekend entrepreneurs featured in the idea chapters? One energetic, creative, and just downright smart bunch of folks! We'd like you to meet one last weekend entrepreneur, who we think possesses all of these stellar qualities.

"At four years old I knew I wanted to be a world-famous singer! I don't know how I actually came up with that idea but I was absolutely certain that singing was what I wanted to do. I remember standing in front of my bedroom mirror with my brush (microphone) in my right hand and a blanket tied around my head (I wanted to have long hair like the rock stars) pretending I was a big star on a huge stage (like Madison Square Garden) jamming on a rock song and thousands of fans chanting my name in total adoration!" Today, New York City-based Delilah Tollinchi is a 25-year-old singer/songwriter whose music definitely reflects her Latin roots.

Delilah's vocal style has been described as "powerful" and critics and audiences agree that this diminutive diva has a big voice that "packs a punch!" After majoring in voice at the fabled Music and Art High School (you know it from TV and the movies; it was the "Fame" school), Delilah put her singing aspirations on hold until after college. She recently received stellar accolades for a gospel performance with Patti Labelle and Billy Preston during the closing ceremonies of the Liberty Celebration.

For the past year Delilah, like many other ambitious weekend entrepreneurs, has been working Monday through Friday at her day job in a media company. Yet, when Friday strikes, she hits the road with the coverband she performs with. They travel to clubs in Atlantic City, Pennsylvania, Connecticut, Maryland, and Detroit. "I belt out 30 songs in three to four hours a night for three nights in a row with very little sleep. In other words, I've been working seven days a week straight." With no time left to take her singing career to the next level, she recently decided to leave the coverband to focus on her original music while she continues working as an editorial assistant for *Fortune Small Business* magazine, a Time, Inc., subsidiary.

Now that Delilah realizes that she's gotten all she needed out of performing on the road, she can move on. And with a new found sense of confidence she is ready for uncharted waters as a solo artist. "I'd rather be singing my original songs at some dive club in New York City for no money, than to belt three hours worth of cover songs at a gig in Atlantic City for about $200. Cover gigs are just not worth it anymore."

While many entrepreneurs have a side business to earn extra cash to build their nest eggs, Delilah takes every buck she earns from singing and puts it right back into the business. "When I first decided to seriously pursue my dream career as a singer, I had no idea what I was getting myself into." She has a long list of expenditures that include buying special clothes for her performances, and personal necessities like hair, makeup, manicures, pedicures, and waxing to general things like photos, her web site, vocal training, acting classes, subscriptions to trade papers, musician's salaries, and studio rentals. One of her streams of income is from her CD that she sells at her solo gigs. "I released an acoustic demo of four original songs, just vocals and acoustic guitar. It cost me $2,000 to make plus $250 for the guitarist's fee and travel expenses." Check it out at www.delilahsdomain.com.

We think you will agree with us—Delilah is a woman of great courage and an amazing example to anyone who has a passion that he or she has chosen to ignore or put on the back burner. She shared this powerful message with us: "Some people have said I'm running out of time as the years go by. Some say if I haven't made it by now, I probably won't. Some people think that music is something I just do on the side as a hobby. Some say I shouldn't waste time on such a foolish dream. Some say that there are tons of singers out there just as good or better than me. I say that I'm living the life of a singer/songwriter and so I'm already a success, whether or not I make it big. I say that I am living the life others dream of. I say I have the courage to pursue my dreams. I say my day job is what I do on the side! I say that all the good things in my life have happened later. I say that I sing with raw passion, power, guts, and soul! I say that I made a four-year-old little girl's dream come true!"

Do you see yourself in Delilah's hopes and dreams? In her hard work and determination? In a job market where so many are feeling lost and unsatisfied at work, where pay scales aren't rising, and 7.6 million Americans are unemployed, isn't it high time we start exploring other alternatives to solidify our wealth, our success, and our future? Your journey begins with the first step. Even if you don't know exactly what kind of a side business you want to start, just knowing that you want more is enough.

If you are on the verge of becoming a weekend entrepreneur you can start by asking yourself this question: "If I could do whatever I want and money wasn't an issue, what sort of business would I start?"

Discovering what you have a passion for can help you select a category for a business; it could be a hobby, a natural talent, or something you have favored since childhood. Many of the *Weekend Entrepreneur* stories we discovered had the following things in common:

- People who started a side business purely out of necessity. They recognized a good idea when they saw it and seized the opportunity when it appeared.
- Some had a hobby or an area of interest, and the need to pursue that passion was so strong that they were compelled to follow their hearts even if it meant going in a direction other than their college degrees.
- Others created their weekend businesses as extensions of their day jobs. Realizing they could make extra money using their expertise, they began getting clients or created a product and voila, they were in business, some in a relatively short amount of time!
- They were fascinated with business opportunities they learned about mainly because it fit their lifestyles and didn't

take a lot of money to launch so they decided to take action and got started.

Did this book appeal to you because you are unhappy at work, in your day job? Deciding to become a weekend entrepreneur can be a way to re-energize yourself and add much-needed excitement and growth to your life. Instead of spending eight hours a day at a job that you don't enjoy, you can focus that energy into trying to spot small ways to create a part-time business around what you already know.

Bloggers Rule

Many of the businesses we covered here could benefit by blogging, creating buzz and interest online, and in turn, raising the profile of the business. You've read about blogging in the newspaper, in magazines, and heard about it from your friends, but has anyone actually explained what it is and how to do it? And better yet, how it can help market and publicize your part-time endeavors?

Jill Hart, founder and editor of Christian Work at Home Moms, CWAHM.com, has a web site dedicated to providing moms with free resources to aid them in their work-at-home search. She is also a blogger who happily shares what she knows.

"It seems everyone these days is talking about blogging. Everywhere I go, I find articles and forums devoted to this craze. I also have heard from many moms who are trying to figure out what a blog is and how they can use one to their benefit. The term "blog" is short for "weblog," which just means an online journal or "log." You can jot down personal thoughts and notes, post articles you've written, or keep track of interesting web sites you find. The sky is the limit, it seems, when it comes to blogging. A blog is something entirely of your own creation and you can use it to share your thoughts with the world; well . . . with anyone you can get to read it anyway.

Blogging

On the internet, blog (short for weblog) is a personal journal or newsletter that usually represents the personality of the writer or the web site and is updated frequently. Updating a blog is "blogging" and someone who keeps a blog is a "blogger." Blogs are typically updated daily using software that allows people with little or no technical background to maintain the blog.

Blog scripting allows you to automatically post information to a web site. The written content first goes to a blogger web site, then it is automatically inserted into a template tailored for your web site.

There are several free blogs including Goggle's www.blogger.com.

One of the main debates going on about blogs is whether blogging can be done to improve search engine rankings for businesses or to create a buzz about business web sites. Both of these can be true if the blog is used correctly. Many resources show that once a blog is created, many times it is listed in search engines within 48 hours. This was true of the blog I created for Christian Work at Home Moms.

There are many ways to create a blog. The easiest by far is to use one of the free tools available online, such as Google's blogger. Jennifer used blogspot.com to create her blog, The Black Dress Manifesto at http://blackdressmanifesto.blogspot.com. You can create your blog for free using their online tools and templates (nothing to download). After you have created the blog, you can then publish your blog through them and your blog is posted online for the world to see.

Jill points out that once you've created your blog, you will need to decide how you will use it. Will it be a personal blog, full of thoughts and comments for yourself alone or maybe your family? Or will it be a business blog, with articles and tips for potential customers? If you want your blog to be found by others, blogging experts recommend that you begin by setting the title and descriptions for your blog. These are similar to the title and descriptions you set for your web site. Try to make them meaningful because they are what people will see when your blog is returned in a search engine. If your description is simply "my blog," you may not draw the attention you'd like.

If you are blogging in the hopes of attracting customers, make sure to use wise use of words and links in your blogs. Try to avoid the "click here" link. Instead, opt for links within descriptive sentences. Add the HTML link within the sentence and attach it to the words that are closely related to the page or site you are linking to. Jills says to link to her web site she would not use "click here" as the link, "I would say, "Please visit Christian Work at Home Moms for homebased work resources."

There are many ways to use a blog for business use. If used correctly, a blog can be a terrific tool to inform potential customers of your business. Be sure to update your blog at least once a week so that the content remains fresh and you remain in the search engines. Blog on!

Protecting Your Products

Some of the weekend entrepreneurs we featured here had invented or developed new products. If this is a route that appeals to you, there are a few warnings along the way. Not only can your designs and ideas be swiped by others, there are many unscrupulous folks out there waiting to take financial advantage of naïve inventors.

Patents and Trademarks

To protect your invention—whether it is a process, design, formula, service, or product—you need a patent. A trademark, on the other hand, is a system of words or logos that represent a product or service. Patents protect ideas, while trademarks protect the way those ideas are brought to the marketplace.

Entrepreneur magazine is a savvy source of up-to-date information on the patent process; you can find more information at their web site, www.entrepeneur.com. You can also go straight to the web site of the U.S. Patent and Trademark Office at www.uspto.gov.

Licensing

Once you have a valid U.S. patent, you will want to license—not sell—your designs to the company that will manufacture, market, and sell them. In a license deal, you grant a company the right to make and sell your product, and they pay you a royalty (usually 1 or 2 percent of the retail price) on each sale. So far, so good. But how do you go about getting a license deal, especially when you have limited resources? Is there anyone out there who can help you license your product?

According to Mark Nowotarski, a patent agent and founder of Markets, Patents and Alliances LLC in Stamford, Connecticut, (www.marketsandpatents.com), there are two types of people who help inventors land license deals—licensing agents and invention promotion firms—but you have to be careful. "Invention promotion firms are those companies you see advertising on television at two o'clock in the morning," says Nowotarski, "and they have a very bad reputation for being misleading about what they will do for their clients."

That leaves licensing agents. Nowotarski says that for consumer products such as handbags, the best place to look for licensing agents is in the classified ads section of *Inventor's Digest* magazine (www.inventorsdigest.com). According to Nowotarski, a typical licensing agent will work either for an hourly fee or an upfront payment of "a couple of thousand dollars—anything more than that and I would be suspicious of their intentions," and will want a percentage (up to 50 percent) of the royalty you receive from the manufacturer.

Nowotarski also recommends attending your local chapter meeting of the Licensing Executives Society (www.usa-canada .les.org). While the Society's members focus on high-tech products—pharmaceuticals, electronics, and telecommunications rather than consumer goods, Nowotarski explains that "Society members usually know 'who's who in the zoo,' and can direct you to some local licensing agents with solid reputations."

Before approaching a licensing agent, though, you need to do some basic market research: Just saying you envision your products in Wal-Mart or Target stores isn't enough. Here's a suggestion from Nowotarski: Go to a local university and ask the engineering department to make a prototype of your product as a student project, without charge to you. Then pay a local manufacturer to make a small "trial run," say, a couple of hundred units. Then, sell your product on eBay and see what happens. "You won't make a lot of money," says Nowotarski, "but you will find out what parts of the country are interested and what the retail price might be. That kind of market intelligence will make it a lot easier for your agent to narrow down the list of potential buyers and quickly help you land the right licensing deal."

Before hiring a licensing agent, Nowotarski insists you speak to inventors the agent has dealt with in the past, and trust your gut instincts: "There's never a free lunch in the licensing business; if an agent promises you one, walk away."

On Your Mark, Get Set, GO!

The last few pages are filled with yellow flags of caution, reminding you to take the proper steps necessary to make sure your ideas don't get ripped off in your weekend pursuits. Enough of the yellow caution flag we've been waving here; you can now picture us both—Michelle and Jennifer—smiling at the starting line, ready to drop that green flag and start you off on the road to an extra income.

We hope that we have opened your eyes and your mind to the amazing possibilities that exist for creating extra money in your spare time. If you didn't find the right idea here, take your new way of thinking and look more closely at the world around you. There is an idea for a part-time business out there for you.

Why not find a buddy to join with you in looking for an opportunity? Business expert Richard Beaty advises budding entrepreneurs to create a mastermind group for support and inspiration; find people who are successful and copy them, and invest in your business and marketing education. Meet once a week over coffee to discuss articles you've read in the newspaper about emerging trends, interesting businesses you've spotted in your daily routine, or ideas that have popped into your head. Bounce it all off your business buddies, and listen carefully to what they have to share about their ideas and observations. Two imaginations are better than one, and could lead you both to the perfect part-time business. Get busy and use the creativity God gave you.

Are you holding yourself back because of past failures? If you are one of those people who jumps on the bandwagon every time a new seminar or business opportunity comes to town, you may be derailing your success. If you have tried and failed in business, or if you have a tendency to get excited about having your dream business but then never take action, do not be discouraged. You are not preordained to failure. There are countless examples in business of entrepreneurs who had to try several different things and experience set backs before finding the right fit. Remember, Colonel Sanders was well up in years before he finally founded Kentucky Fried Chicken! Don't give up your dreams.

OK, are you ready? Start up your creative business engine, put your foot on the gas pedal of life, and GO!

9

SPREAD THE WORD
Effectively Publicizing and
Marketing Your Business

You've now met over 100 people with amazing stories of success to share. The difficult truth is that for every one of those enterprising entrepreneurs, there is a good chance that someone else tried a similar idea, and failed. Why does one small business catch on and succeed, while another seems to sink into obscurity? One simple word—publicity. No, wait! Let's make that two simple words—*free publicity*!

pub·lic·i·ty			
a.	Information that concerns a person, group, event, or product and that is disseminated through various media to attract public notice.		
b.	Public interest, notice, or notoriety achieved by the spreading of such information.		
c.	The act, process, or occupation of disseminating information to gain public interest.		

Source: www.dictionary.com

Publicity is free—unlike advertising or marketing, there is no dollar cost attached to it. Publicity is a newspaper story, a magazine article, a television or radio spot in which you and your business are featured. Potential customers trust publicity more than they trust advertising, and you need to go after it as often as you can! There really is no such thing as *too much* publicity!

We also have several other inexpensive marketing techniques to share later in the chapter. There are powerful strategies that weekend entrepreneurs can benefit from, if only they knew how to find the information. You will learn closely-guarded secrets from industry insiders as well as tips from business people who know shortcuts to getting maximum exposure for your business, product, service, or message. Let's start off with the power of television

As Seen on TV!

For many years Michelle was the Executive Producer of "The Dr. Laura Show," as well as a producer on television shows like *Leeza*, and *A&E Biography*, and as a freelance associate producer on *The Oprah Winfrey Show*. She has seen firsthand the dramatic effect that publicity can have on business success. "I've seen small entrepreneurs be interviewed, go home, and learn that their businesses have literally jumped 100 fold in the time it took them to get home! They discover phones ringing off the hook, e-mail boxes flooded with orders, and even better—there are calls from more producers and reporters who also want to do a story on them! It breeds both new business and new interest in further publicity," she says.

Television is one of the most powerful mediums and one of the most effective communication tools in the world. Its visual images capture our imagination and bring us together as a community the way nothing else does. It's not unusual for public relations folks and marketing experts alike to give advice on how to get free publicity by being on the evening news. You need to learn how to use television to your advantage in publicizing your weekend business.

Our belief is that if you want to learn the right way to approach this medium, then we recommend you get your information straight from the experts. TV producers Alison Woo and Sandy Coots have over 25 years of television news experience. They have both created thousands of hours of programs and have experienced the power of television close-up and personal, and together they created a handbook about how you can get your message across succinctly and efficiently to the people who can get your message on TV. You can learn more about it at www.tvsavvy.com, but they have generously agreed to give our readers a glimpse of their expert advice.

Alison and Sandy learned these well-kept secrets while working in the trenches as producers and managers in newsrooms around the nation. Their real-life experience taught them that there are amazing stories in our communities, but there's a real challenge in finding them. Alison Woo is a former Executive Producer at News 14 Carolina, a Time-Warner 24-hour news station in Charlotte, North Carolina. She has worked for *CNN Headline News*, Emmy-award winning anchor Linda Ellerbee, and freelances for national news organizations, including MSNBC.com.

Sandy Coots specializes in both field and line producing, from concept to completion. She has worked for WXYZ, WNEM, and WJRT in Michigan. She still freelances for those stations as well as national news organizations including *ABC News*, *NBC News*, and *MSNBC*.

Impressive experts, both, and anxious to help you learn how to get the message out about your new business. Read along and learn the inside tricks on getting you and your business booked quickly.

From Pitch to Package

For every great story idea or brilliant caller, there are at least a dozen bad ideas and somewhat certifiable people who call any TV station. That's why many news people are skeptical when answering the newsroom phone. So, you need to know what questions to ask to find the individual most likely to facilitate getting you on TV.

Who You Gonna Call?

If you answered "Ghostbusters" you're probably movie fans like us, but knowing whom to talk to is vital.

The first step is knowing the appropriate person to whom you need to pitch your story idea. The anchors are the most well-known members of the newsroom, but they rarely have anything to do with choosing the stories that are covered.

The three key decision-makers in getting stories on the air are: the producers (lead by the Executive Producer), the assignment desk (led by the Assignment Desk Manager), and the reporters (usually lead by the Managing Editor or the Assistant News Director).

Producers

The producer (sometimes called a line producer) is the person who runs each individual show. It's her responsibility to make sure the show has the right amount of content. She is responsible for filling the news hole, which is the length of the show minus the number of commercials. The news hole can vary from day to day depending on commercials, editorials, or other programming situations, but a typical 30-minute show will have about 8 minutes of commercials so they need about 22 minutes of editorial content.

The Executive Producer is the news manager usually in charge of a certain time of day. He supervises the producers and they, in concert with the Assignment Manager, are the key decision makers to what stories actually go on the air, especially the stories the reporters will do and where the stations will be live in the field.

The best way to contact producers is to call when they are in the building. AND, it's important to know what kind of story you are pitching. The station's morning show is typically the place for interview segments and lighter material. If your story idea fits this mold, you'll need to contact the morning show producer. E-mail is perfectly acceptable and a great alternative, especially if you tend to get tongue-tied, but you'll need to provide that producer with your contact information. A little lead-time is also helpful. Typically morning show producers are scheduling interview segments and guests a couple of days or weeks in advance. Do not e-mail the morning show producer about your event the night before it is supposed to happen. That is most likely to end up as a wasted opportunity. Give yourself at least a two-week leadtime.

Assignment Desk Staff

The assignment desk staff are often called "gatekeepers" because they filter most of the newsroom's calls every day. Assignment editors really do not like to be bothered with people who don't know what they want. They view the phone as an intrusion. After all, it's their job to get crews to the stories that need to be covered. They are responsible for people flow. The phone is not a good conduit for people flow. If you call the news-room, call early in the morning or after lunch. This is likely to be the least hectic time. If you have questions, make sure the list is short. Be polite and courteous. It really can help.

Reporters

Reporters are always looking for story ideas. Reporters are the station's faces and storytellers. You can usually find a way to contact a reporter from the station's web site. Most stations have a biography page and a "contact me" link listed on the biography page. When you e-mail a reporter, make your request succinct, don't be wordy. And, make sure you include contact information, a phone number is important. Do not simply expect a return e-mail. The reporter might have questions that would need to be answered before considering pursuing your idea.

You may also try calling the station's switchboard. Some stations do allow the switchboard operator to provide information, direct dial phone numbers, e-mail addresses, or even work hours. If the switchboard operator won't give you an e-mail address, try going to the station's web site. Most stations list reporter biographies on their web sites and from there you can often figure out another employee's e-mail address.

Persistence is always good, pestering not so much. A little flattery may be okay, but don't go overboard. Producers and reporters alike do not appreciate being played/set-up. Wait a couple of days after submitting an idea. If you call or e-mail too often you will be branded as a stalker and then anything you say or submit will rarely be seriously considered.

Greg Pallone is a reporter for the CBS affiliate in Atlanta, Georgia. He says he gets story ideas all the time and prefers either e-mail or phone. "The key thing is be brief," he said. "I need to get the gist of the story in 30 seconds. What you'll most likely hear from me is that I need to check with the higher ups and sell them on the story." He also says you can definitely follow up, but don't be a pest.

When dealing with any news employee, it's important to know what you're going to say before you pick up the phone. Imagine being on the other end of this call:

Station: "Eyewitness News, this is Mary. How can I help you?"

Caller: "Um, hi."

Station: "Hi."

Caller: "I'd like to be on the news."

Station: "Do you have a story?"

Caller: "Yup."

Station: "OK, what is it?"

Caller: "Well, I don't know. I'm not sure if it's very good but I watch you guys all the time. You're my favorite station."

Station: "Thanks. What's your story?"

Caller: "I work downtown and I have a dog. He's a really great dog . . . a golden retriever. Do you have a dog?"

Station: "Um, no."

Caller: "Well, my dog used to bark all the time. I 'd come home and my neighbors used to give me weird looks. I live in south Brunswick. That's on the east side near where the old mill used to be. Do you know where that is?"

Station: "Um, yeah. Do you have a story?"

Caller: "Well, yeah. After a couple of times I got home I realized that my dog needed a companion. He wouldn't stop barking. But I couldn't get another dog. My wife would kill me. So I designed a great new gizmo that sounds just like another dog." (Pause)

Station: "Uh, huh."

> *Caller:* "Well now it's selling on internet."
>
> *Station:* "Well, thanks for calling us. Good luck with that."
> (Click)

Don't laugh. A lot of calls sound like that and worse. Clearly, that didn't go very well. The caller was unfocused and Mary felt like that was a major waste of time. If she hears his voice again, she'll be sure to give him the brush off ASAP.

Now, see what happens when you're savvy.

> *Station:* "Eyewitness News, this is Mary. How can I help you?"
>
> *Caller:* "Hi, I'd like to talk with the Producer for the 5:30 show."
>
> *Station:* "That's will be Mark. Hold on, I'll transfer you."
>
> *Mark:* "Hi, this is Mark."
>
> *Caller:* "Hi Mark, I'm a viewer who's been watching your stories on the city council's battle to crack down on noisy dogs. My company developed a product so now dog owners don't have to give up their dogs or muzzle them when they're away at work. We're setting up a doggie booth right in downtown right outside City Hall next week on the day the city's set to make their final decision. Can I send you some information about it?"
>
> *Mark:* "Yeah, that would be great."
>
> *Caller:* "What's your e-mail address or fax?"
>
> *Mark:* "It's mark@anytstation.com and our fax is (555) 555-1212."
>
> *Caller:* "We'll have a lot of people who'll be bringing their dogs and have been really upset. We'll be right next door to City Hall so it's convenient for you guys if you want to interview them. I can even set you up with some of them."

Mark:	"That would be great. What time is the booth going to be open?"
Caller:	"From 4 to 7 P.M."
Mark:	"Wow, we could even go live from the booth. OK, I want you to also send your information to our Assignment Manager and our Managing Editor so we can get a reporter assigned to your story. Thanks a lot!"

OK, that went a lot differently than the first call. Why? Because the caller had a focus. He knew exactly whom he needed to talk to. Second, the caller was brief and to the point. He set up the parameters of why he was calling, what benefit it had to the viewers, and pegged it to a story that was timely. People who work in the news don't have the time or desire to find the hook for every story. You have to make it clear from the onset. Next, notice the caller didn't give you details of how he developed the product, what the product was exactly, or even how it worked, but gave enough of a feel that the producer was intrigued. He wanted to find out more. That's how every great news tease works.

Other smart points: He set up the event, the doggie booth, at a location that is easily accessible to news crews and on a day when news stations would want to advance that story, as well as setting up at a key time so that they could be live during the 5 to 6:30 P.M. newscast. Another key point not to be missed: Our entrepreneur said that he would have people that the company could talk to. So picture the visuals here, you've got dogs, you've got the device, you've got unhappy owners now made happy by the product; this is primo placement at its best! And you can't pay for this kind of placement. Now all the caller has to do is contact the other two or three stations in his city and he has a home run. That's what we're talking about when we say being TV savvy!

You could do the same thing with e-mail. Just make it short, make it compelling, and please put a catchy subject line like:

Local company comes up with solution for noisy dog problem.

Best Times to Contact a News Station

The beauty of e-mail is that it's 24/7, so feel free to send it anytime. But if you're going to call, please remember that news stations are *very* busy around news time. That means calling between 4 and 7 A.M., 11 A.M. to 1P.M., and 3:30 to 7 P.M., or 10 to 11 P.M. are not good times. That's the usual guideline. If there's a breaking news story and you have a great hook to it, call, but please state that fact in the first ten seconds, because the reporters, producers, assignment editors, photographers, and anyone else in the newsroom are busy trying to get things ready for the show. It's a very chaotic time.

You can make e-mail and faxes work for you. The key is sending them to the right person. When faxes come in, they are scanned for a name. If it's not sent to someone in particular, then whoever grabs it will determine if it's an idea the station might want to cover. And, it's important to note, different people view ideas differently. A morning show producer might see the value in a book tour about do-it-yourself housewives, the 6 P.M. producer probably would not.

How to Find Out Whom to Call

Back in the day, stations used to run credits behind each show so you could see who was involved with the show. Now that timing is everything and everyone wants to seamlessly transition from one show to another, the credits are mostly gone. It's a lot easier with reporters because they are on-air and chances are you already know their names. But you may just have to pick up the phone and ask, "Who is the Executive Producer for the morning show? Who's the Assignment Manager for the weekend shows?"

You can also go to a great TV web site called TV Jobs (www.tvjobs.com). They have a treasure trove of information on local TV stations all over the country. You don't need a subscription for that page and you'll find out station addresses, phone numbers, faxes, and names of key personnel. We suggest you call and double-check that that information is still current. TV is a very dynamic medium and people change jobs frequently, so call to make sure that that person is still there. Also, no one wants to receive a fax sent to: 5 P.M. Producer. Think about how you feel when you get a letter in the mail that says: Dear Occupant. It makes you mad. And in TV, just as in life, it's the little things that count!

Getting on TV is really not as difficult as it may seem, and you don't need to spend thousands of dollars to do it. Being on local TV newscasts is *FREE!* How much more can you ask for?

What's the downside? Control. When you tell your story to a journalist, you don't have control over the final product. You don't know how much of your story is going to be told, in what order, or when. But by *being TV savvy* and really understanding the TV medium, you'll have a better understanding of why telling your story to some channels may be better for you than others. There's a whole untapped world of potential waiting for you. Remember that TV news professionals need your story just as much as you need to share it. There are lots of ways to be on TV; for additional information visit their web site at www.tvsavvy.com .

Marketing with Instant Messaging

Now that you have the secrets of getting to the right producers and booking yourself on TV, what other ways can you spread the

Instant Messaging

The new "three-foot rule" in business is "When you're siting in front of your computer, you're within three feet of the entire online world." You can talk to anyone when you know where to find them and how to use Instant Messaging (IM).

Using IM can put you in contact with people everywhere in the world. It gives you direct access to millions of new people.

word on your business? Here's a new way—did you know that on any given day, millions log on to use instant messaging (IM)? Why not harness IM to get your message out to potential customers?

If you know your way around the internet, then you know how popular IM is. Max Steingart has been the Internet Mentor for the network marketing industry since 1997 and shares a dynamic new way to find people who are looking for your product or service. And you can use this breakthrough technique which has been used socially for years. The following comes from Max's book, *Make the Internet Your Warm Market: The Complete Guide to Networking through Instant Messaging*. Also visit his web site at www.successway.com.

Instant Messaging and the new Three-Foot Rule
by Max Steingart

Finding someone to talk to about your business is a lot simpler than you think when you know how to use IM on the internet.

If, like most business professionals, you've exhausted your warm market (all the people you know) and now depend on talking to anyone within three feet of you that could be interested in your business, you're going to fall in love with IM.

If you're brand new to sales or need to find new clients, and you're struggling with your first assignment—make a list of everyone you know so you can tell them about your business—your worries are over. IM solves your problem by giving you direct access to millions of new people.

Now, you can roll up your sleeves and get to work building your business with a smile. IM will put you in direct contact with people everywhere in the world. You should be using it to talk to people that you know and you can use it to talk to strangers.

You'll make the internet your warm market when you use IM. The new "three-foot rule" in business is: When you're sitting in front of your computer, you're within three feet of the entire online world. You can talk to anyone when you know where to find them and how to use IM.

The internet and IM made all the difference in Melanie Rogers' success.

Melanie was a young woman living in central Canada. She didn't have a warm market to talk to. Her chiropractor suggested she send out promotional audiotapes to a mailing list she purchased. Every week for an entire year, she mailed out ten tapes to different people on the list and every week she thought "One of these people is going to listen to the tape and call me," but no one ever did.

Melanie heard that other people in her company were using IM to meet people online to talk about their business. She asked her friend if he knew how people were using the internet, but he didn't have a clue. So she traveled to an event sponsored by her company in Chicago, to meet other distributors and to learn how they were using the internet.

Melanie met Angela waiting for an elevator at her hotel. Angela knew all about internet prospecting. "I'm meeting six people who I met online, at this hotel later today. They're considering getting into my business," she told Melanie. "Come up to my room during lunch and I'll show you how easy it is to send an IM to a total stranger and establish a relationship."

Later in Angela's room, Melanie watched in amazement as her new friend used a laptop to search the Member Directory in Yahoo! and ICQ, two of the world's largest free IM systems. She saw Angela pick from hundreds of people who were online and start an IM conversation with someone that lived close to the hotel. Before the online conversation ended, Angela's new friend made a commitment to stop by the hotel later to meet her and learn more about the business.

When Melanie returned home from Chicago, she immediately began her internet adventure. She created the screen name Marvelous Melanie and posted a fabulous profile in the Member Directory on Yahoo!. She wanted to use the internet to meet people in the cities where her company held promotional events. The company's next event was in Orlando, Florida, and Melanie planned to attend.

Melanie learned a lot about her business and company's products in Chicago. She made many new friends and had a fun-filled weekend. She learned new skills that she would apply to her business, but the biggest thing she learned was how to use the internet and IM.

Melanie searched the Member Directory looking for people to contact in Orlando. She started every IM conversation with:

Hello, My name is Melanie. I'm coming to Orlando at the end of January for a convention. Do you know what the temperature will be there then? I'm in Canada and expect it will be 5 or 10 below zero here.

Melanie made 20 new contacts that turned into friends in the Orlando area with these initial IMs. Six of these friends became customers prior to the convention and attended it with her. Two of the six were chiropractors. Before she left town, she added an additional six clients from her new contact list.

A year and a half later, when Melanie's company expanded into the United Kingdom, she immediately started making new friends in London. She started each IM with a compliment and a reference to the contents of the person's profile.

Hello, I like your profile. I'm coming to London at the end of July for a five-day convention. My company is expanding our business there. How difficult is it to get a tour of Buckingham Palace? I'd really appreciate your help.

Melanie made six good friends in London and made plans to meet them when she was there.

On her first day in London, Melanie met her new internet friends and they all got involved in her business. The first client she got was the head coach of a professional soccer team. He convinced everyone connected with his team that they needed to be taking the company's products and all of them became her customers.

As a result, Melanie became her company's first national marketing rep in the United Kingdom. A woman with zero sales activity the first year she was in business found incredible success on the internet.

Effective use of IM solves the biggest problem facing everyone building their business. It provides access to millions of people and makes the internet YOUR warm market.

Marketing with Coupons

Let's step away from technology for a moment and go back to the days when mom clipped coupons to save a couple of bucks when she was going shopping at the supermarket. Today that money-saving trend is every bit as appealing to entice business people and consumers as it was to our parents when we were growing up.

Can you see your new weekend business working in a coupon? It could be a great way to get the word out fast on your service or product. To get the latest tips on how you can use coupons to accelerate your growth we turned to Thom Reece, CEO and creator of a direct response marketing company called the Online Marketing Resource Center, http://www.e-comprofits.com.

Facts about Coupons

Ninety-five percent of all shoppers like coupons and 60 percent actively look for coupons. *Source*: A.C. Nielsen Company.

Coupons "pull in the business." They have gained remarkable acceptance and popularity among astute marketing managers.

Coupons will entice new customers who have been shopping at your competitor.' It's a proven fact that consumers will break routine shopping patterns to take advantage of a good coupon offer.

Put the Profit-Producing Power of Coupons to Work

Coupons have proven themselves to be highly effective sales tools for every conceivable size and type of business. Because coupons "pull in the business," they have gained remarkable acceptance and popularity among astute marketing managers. A simple explanation for their acceptance by advertisers is their overwhelming acceptance and use by the consuming public. In fact, *Advertising Age* (the bible of the advertising industry) reports that 87 percent of all shoppers use coupons.

Another independent marketing research firm, the A.C. Nielson Co., reveals that 95 percent of all shoppers like coupons. And 60 percent actively look for coupons. A recent article in *The Wall Street Journal* entitled, "In a Pinch, Snip," states that coupon use rises as the economy in any given area slides. Of the shoppers surveyed, 54 percent said they had already stepped up use of coupons, and even more are expected to do so.

It's very easy to see why coupon advertising is sweeping the country. Regular use of good couponing strategy will provide a steady stream of new customers and high quality sales leads. Savvy marketers cite these reasons for heavy reliance on couponing:

- Coupons have the effect of expanding or increasing your market area. We know that consumers will travel far to redeem a valuable coupon.
- Coupons will entice new customers that have been shopping at your competitors'. It's a proven fact that consumers will break routine shopping patterns to take advantage of a good coupon offer.
- Coupons attract new residents when they are actively in the market for products and services.
- Coupons will re-activate old customers. Those customers that have been lured away by your competitor will start buying from you again when you give them a good reason to do so.
- Coupon advertising provides the opportunity for additional profits through sale of related items. (Business owners often forget this.) When you offer a special "deal" on a coupon to invite a customer to do business with you, you have to remember that this same customer will probably

end up buying additional items that carry a full profit margin. In addition, you also are being given the opportunity to "sell-up" to a more profitable product or service. You would not have had this opportunity had it not been for the coupon getting the customer through the door in the first place.

- Coupons build store traffic which results in additional impulse purchases.
- Coupons are measurable and accountable. Don't overlook that couponing is the most measurable and accountable form of promotion.

It's simply a matter of counting the number of coupons redeemed to judge the effectiveness of the offer. Wise use of this consumer feedback will guide you in creating future offers that improve your results.

Understand that the media delivering the coupon has very little to do with the response. Publications simply deliver your offer to a specific audience. It's up to you to determine what offer produces the best response from that audience. You do this through methodically testing various offers. Savvy use of this "coupon-testing" technique will give you the specific knowledge you require to greatly improve all of your advertising responses, your sales, and your profits.

How do you go about creating a coupon promotion that will work for YOU? Here's what Thom calls his 12 Tips for Effective Couponing:

Tip 1: Make a Solid Offer

- *Offer discounts.* "$50 off!," "60 percent off!," Percentage discounts are only good when they are high percentages and the value of the product or service is well known. "Dollars Off" discounts work best.

- *Offer bonuses.* "Buy One/Get One Free!" "Two Free with Each Case Ordered!" "Free Batteries When You Buy One Super Flashlight" or "Free Drop Cloth with Each Gallon of Super Paint," etc.
- *Offer premiums.* Offer premiums for a presentation, for a trial order, for a subscription, for a demonstration, for a new customer referral, for an order amounting to $xxx or larger."
- *Offer free information.* "FREE booklet," "FREE brochure," "FREE estimate," "FREE details," "FREE samples," "FREE trial," "FREE consultation," "FREE quote," etc.

Tip 2: Use Bold, Commanding, and Specific Headlines
- "Save $50 on any Portable TV . . . This Month Only!"
- "FREE BROCHURE . . . 'Beauty Secrets for Career Woman'"
- "Free Catalog Saves YOU 70 Percent on Office Supplies!"
- "Rent Two NEW RELEASE Video Movies—Get One FREE!"
- "Buy One Dinner Entree—Get One FREE!"
- "Buy Five Cases of Copier Paper—Get the Sixth Case Absolutely Free!"

Tip 3: Use Line Illustrations or Photographs
- Illustrations work best when you show products in use.
- Illustrations enhance credibility, aid understanding, and create desire.

Tip 4: Use Your Logo in Your Coupon
- Use of your logo builds company identity and awareness in the marketplace, enhances your image, lends credibility to your offer, and improves response.

Tip 5: Make Effective Use of White Space
- Don't clutter. Don't cram.

Tip 6: Sell the Benefits

- Save time, save money, increase profits, protect your family, improve your standard of living, be happier, improve your health, increase your income, increase your comfort, more convenient, etc.

Tip 7: Appeal to the Self-Interest of Your Customer

- Your customer is only interested in what you can do for him or her. Your customer will only buy the benefits-of-use of your product or service. Let me say that again . . . your customer is only interested in the benefits of use of your product . . . not the product itself.

Tip 8: Make Effective Use of the 18 Most Powerful Words in Advertising

- Free, now, new, how to, save, guarantee, money, easy, simple, you, proven, love, results, discovery, fast, amazing, sex, profit.

Tip 9: Always Up-Sell

- Offer extras when a customer requests information or places an order. Always suggest related items. Point out the added features and benefits of a higher-priced item and then show the customer specifically how these features will make his life easier, safer, etc.

Tip 10: Spread Your Specials Around—Consider the Traffic Pattern in a Retail Store

- Set up product displays so that you force your customer to walk the entire expanse of your store. Your "impulse" buys will increase dramatically when you expose your customer to more products by well planned placement of "sale items."

Tip 11: Capture Your Customer's Name, Address, and Telephone Number. Develop an In-House Mailing List for On-Going Direct Marketing Use

- Your customer list represents your most valuable asset. Your greatest potential for sales and profits lies in the customer database. To ignore this potential is pure folly.

Tip 12: Don't Stop after the Sale

- Create a planned program of continuous follow-up to your customer list.
- Use ride-alongs, invoice stuffers, new catalogs, new product brochures, special sale fliers, preferred customer sales and discounts, customer appreciation events, more coupons. Keep your customers coming back to YOU!

Start Spreading the Word!

OK, now you have three methods of getting the word out on your new business. Will only one work for your type of business? Maybe two? Perhaps all three techniques—television publicity, instant messaging, and coupons could be put to work for your business.

Whichever method you choose, start spreading the word and get the attention you and your business deserve!

SMALL BUSINESS RESOURCES

Affter reading 101 creative ways to make extra money, we don't want you to feel overwhelmed by the thought of actually going out and doing it yourself. Because you aren't really by yourself, are you? At least 101 folks have gone down this road before you (and thousands more that we didn't get to mention), and have left behind a handy trail to follow through to success. And beyond the helpful advice of these intrepid entrepreneurs, there are many helpful organizations and web sites designed with your needs in mind.

Business Plan

Biz Plan It
www.bizplanit.com

The One-Page Business Plan Company
www.onepagebusinessplan.com

Market Research
www.marketresearch.com

SCORE: Counselors to America's Small Business
www.score.org

Business Organizations

Alliance of Business Women International
www.abwi.org

American Business Women's Association
www.abwahq.org

Asssociation for Enterprise Opportunity
www.microenterpriseworks.org

Catalyst (research and advisory organization)
www.catalysstwomen.org

Center for Women's Business Research
www.nfwbo.org

Digital Women
www.digital-women.com

eBay Training

Sydney Johnston offers a FREE course and paid training for making money on e-Bay
http://auction-genius-course.com

Auction Selling on eBay the Lazy Way on Less Than Two Hours a Day (ebook) by Robin Powers
www.auction-diva.com

Speaker's Training and Resources

College Speaker of the Year, James Malinchak, teaches how you can make money speaking at colleges.
www.malinchak.com

Les Brown, Master Speaker Training
http://lesbrown.com

Lee Glickstein, creator of Speaking Circles, The Art of Full Presence Communication.
www.speakingcircles.com

John Childers, Million Dollar Speaker Training
http://johnchilders.com

National Speakers Association
www.nsaspeaker.org

Toastmasters International
http://toastmasters.org

Networking

Business Network International, the world's largest referral organization.
www.BNI.com

Business to business networking using a revolutionary new approach.
www.freedombuildersinc.net

National Association of Women Business Owners (NABO)
www.nawbo.org

National Coalition of 100 Black Women, Inc.
www.ncbw.org

The Brain Exchange is a monthly, open-ended brainstorming group for women. People give and receive support on personal and business issues like relationships, career questions, marketing strategies,

*entrepreneurial ideas, book ideas, etc. Affiliated brainstorming groups
are emerging nationwide all the time.*
http://thebrainexchange.com

U.S. Chamber of Commerce
www.uschamber.com

World Chamber of Commerce Directory, United States and overseas
www.chamberofcommerce.com

*Womens Leadership Exchange offers an unparalleled way for women
to developed strategic alliances and partnerships.*
www.womensleadershipexchange.com

Teen Resouces

The coolest career dream site for teens and 20s.
www.mycoolcareer.com

Wealth Training for Teens
www.teenwealthexplosion.com

Direct Selling Resources

Direct Selling Association
www.dsa.org

Direct Selling Women's Alliance
www.mydsa.org

*FREE resources to build a Party Plan Business, also great for net-
work marketers and MLM companies.*
www.partyplanpeople.com

*Free weekly training teleseminars to boost your income and produc-
tivity, tons of valuable information.*
www.danijohnson.com

Home Business Resources

American Association of Home Based Bussinesses
www.aahbb.org

Home Office Association of America
www.hoaa.com

Small Office and Home Office
www.soho.org

National Association for the Self-Employed
www.nase.org

Home Business Resource
www.homebusinessworks.com

Internet Association of Information Marketers
www.NetAim.Info

Instant Income
Instantincome.com

Victim of a rip-off? File a complaint against a company or individual who rips off consumers.
http://ripoffreport.com

Better Business Bureau
http://bbb.org

Entrepreneur
www.entrepreneur.com

Internet marketing resource center for nonfiction, business, and self help authors.
http://sellmorebooks.com

Royalty Free Digital Stock Photography
www.rubberball.com

Audio, web, and video applications
www.EasyLiveConference.com

Add audio capabilities to your web site and e-mails
www.InstantFlashAudio.com

Convert to MP3 for PCs
www.dbpoweramp.com

Convert to MP3 for MACs
www.hairersoft.com/Amadeus.html

Free conference call bridge lines
www.FreeConference.com

Take money on your web site
www.PayPal.com

Merchant account service
www.Clickbank.com

Take online payments
www.ibill.com

Contact manager
www.ConstantContact.com

Reminder service
www.memotome.com

Web trends
www.trends.net

Internet safety
www.cyberangels.com

Fulfillment services, one order at a time.
www.iFulfill.com

Will print CD/DVD on demand
www.Mixonic.com

Will print on-demand CDs, T-shirts, cups, etc.
and fulfill orders.
www.cafepress.com

Shopping cart system
www.2Checkout.com

Shopping cart system
www.EasyWebAutomation.com

Sell digital products online.
www.Payloadz.com

Sell and distribute your digital products.
http://Clickbank.com/overview.html

Autoresponder service
www.Aweber.com

Autoresponder service
www.GetResponse.com

Free autoresponder
www.FreeAutobot.com

Autoresponder
www.SendFree.com

Transcription service, 24 hour turnaround.
www.IDictate.com

Learn how to do things
http://webmonkey.wired.com/webmonkey

Create your own webforms.
www.Response-o-Matic.com

Remotely hosted variety of CGI scripts.
www.pages.HostedScripts.com

Promote your web site through the ads of others.
www.Google.com/adsense

Identify effective key words for effective search engine placement.
www.GoodKeywords.com

Ask a question.
http://AskDatabase.com

Legal

Legal info
www.findlaw.com

Trademark
www.tmexpress.com

Trademark application online
www.uspto.gov/teas/index.html

Trademark and copyright
www.nolo.com/category/tc_home.html

Copyright
www.benedict.com

Legal resources
www.ilrg.com

Public Relations and Media

Free press release service
www.PRWeb.com

They get approximately 100 requests a week from reporters who need to quote experts.
http://prleads.com

Pay per play publicists, Annie Jennings is a provider of experts to the media.
www.anniejenningspr.com

Penny Sansevieri creates a dynamic internet presence for authors; hire her or she'll show you how to do-it-yourself.
www.amarketingexpert.com

Jess Todtfeld, the "Pitch Doctor"
www.successinmedia.com

Toastmasters International Speaking Club
www.toastmasters.org

Media consultant and business coach, Michelle Anton.
www.michelleanton.com

Online Research Tools

Free five-minute mp3 recordings by phone
www.audlink.com

Find out what search terms people are searching with.
www.wordtracker.com

Search term tool
www.keywordwizard.com

Free and fee survey tool
www.SurveyMonkey.com

Find out what people are looking for.
www.overture.com

Find out what's selling now.
www.clickbank.com/marketplace

Increase your online sales.
www.marketingtips.com

Read all you want from 200 leading publications for only $4.95 a month.
www.KeepMedia.com

Ebook creator
http://EbookGenerator.com

ISBN identifications for publications (apply online).
www.isbn.org/standards/home/isbn/us/secureapp.asp

ISSN identifications for your newsletter publications (apply online for).
www.loc.gov/issn

Publish your ezine articles, submission to sites, indirectly promote yourself.
www.EzineDirector.com

Online survey tools
www.AdvancedSurvey.com

Create custom assessments, make your own client intake forms, self-scoring assessments, and surveys.
www.AssessmentGenerator.com

PDF Creator
www.pdf995.com

Make long URLs shorter
http://Tinyurl.com

Assess link popularity of your web site.
www.LinkPopularityCheck.com

Flash animation characters "real" people.
www.SitePal.com

Assessments of all types
http://home.att.net/~PersonalAssessments/links/index.html

Create your own surveys, order forms, registration forms.
www.FormSite.com

Find out about how stuff works; might help you design your own stuff.
www.HowStuffWorks.com

Affiliate program to make passive income, (click on associates at the bottom of page).
www.Amazon.com

Find things you need at great prices.
www.eBay.com

E-Mail, Faxes

www.FaxAway.com

www.CallWave.com

www.eFax.com

Information

Internet public library
www.ipl.org

Brainstorming Software
www.mindjet.com/us

Teleclasses, free and fee
www.teleclass.com

Self publishing: A source for print-on-demand books — and a way for authors of all kinds to publish and sell their books. They provide free access to on-demand publishing tools for books, e-books, music, images, and calendars.
www.lulu.com

Entrepreneurial training: Wendy Robbins, co-inventor of 'The Tingler' Head Massager has CDs and books on a variety of topics including how to protect your ideas.
http://nowheretomillionaire.com

Entrepreneurial member web site: Leigh Beaty is a marketing expert who shares stories about how people have become highly successful entrepreneurs.
www.successsecretsrevealed.com

Marketing tips for writers: Essential tips for authors by Al Lautenslager, the best-selling co-author of Guerrilla Marketing in 30 Days. *Check out both web sites:*
www.marketforprofits.com/publishingboxset
http://market-for-profits.com

Getting More Clients: Bernadette Doyle says "Stop chasing. Start cultivating." The Client Magnets web site can show you how.
http://clientmagnets.com

How to get grants: "Power Your Business with Free Money," is the perfect resource on finding and writing grants.
GrantMeRich.com

Hollywood marketing mogul, Randall Blaum's stealth marketing secrets machine helps you increase sales.
www.hollywoodmarketingsystem.com

Real Estate Training

G. William Barnett II has FREE real estate training teleseminars.
www.areyoudumbenoughtoberich.com

Larry Goins offers a FREE seven part e-mail course on getting started in real estate.
http://larrygoins.com

Technology Information and Training

Search Engine Optimization (SEO)
www.bradfallon.com
Brad Fallon helped his wife's web site, www.myweddingfavors
.com earn seven figures in its first year. He created "Stomping the Search Engines," a ten-CD recorded seminar on search engine optimization. Also, he is the host of Search Engine Radio; it can be heard at www.seoradio.com.

Blog Expert
http://andywibbels.com
Andy has a free newsletter seminars and CDs. Also, see http://businessblogbasics.com.

Podcasting for iPods
http://podcastingbootcamp.com
Andy Wibbels teaches a seminar, and has an ebook.

Really Simple Syndication (RSS)
http://rssessentials.com
RSS is a web content syndication format. Andy Wibbels provides training and CDs on this important topic.

Telephone

Call waiting so you don't need two phone lines.
www.pagoo.com

Telephone money saver
www.freewebcall.com

Telephone money saver
www.mediaring.com

Telephone money saver (United States only)
www.dialpad.com

Telephone money saver
www.net2phone.com

Tutorials

HTML
www.htmltutorials.ca

The Newbie Club, considered as one of the most respected learning site for beginners.
www.newbieclub.com/?newbie_heaven

Miscellaneous

Doodle, fun when you're bored or stuck.
www.inventionatplay.org

Great when you're stuck.
www.unstuck.com

Financial literacy web site for women.
www.wealthdiva.com

Guerrila Marketing Coach
www.gmarketingcoach.com

Internet marketing for small businesses.
http://antion.com

Publishing consultant and book writing coach, Jennifer Basye Sander.
basyesander@yahoo.com

Shipping materials
www.uline.com

Audio and video packaging DVD, CD, VHS.
www.polylinecorp.com

Kinkos has a pdf-like format (KDF) and has a variety of binding
options. Great way to create a small number of workbooks.
www.Kinkos.com

Easy way to print, bind, and deliver quality documents overnight
right from your PC.
www.mimeo.com

American Writers and Artist Institute with master copywriter
Michael Masterson.
www.awaionline.com

Copywriting with Joe Vitale.
http://mrfire.com

Copywriting services and course.
www.Red-Hot-Copy.com

Self publishing guru Dan Poynter.
www.parapublishing.com

Adobe Acrobat
www.adobe.com

BusinessTVChannel.com is one of the first internet television channels dedicated to small businesses and entrepreneurs. The channel
offers programming with information and resources to help small
business owners, entrepreneurs, and their employees be successful.
http://businesstvchannel.com

INDEX